Searching for Latini

Searching for Latini

Michael Kleine

Parlor Press
West Lafayette, Indiana
www.parlorpress.com

Parlor Press LLC, West Lafayette, Indiana 47906

© 2006 by Parlor Press
All rights reserved.
Printed in the United States of America
S A N: 2 5 4—8 8 7 9

Library of Congress Cataloging-in-Publication Data

Kleine, Michael, 1948-
  Searching for Latini / Michael Kleine.
      p. cm.
  Includes bibliographical references and index.
  ISBN 1-932559-85-X (pbk. : alk. paper) -- ISBN 1-932559-
      86-8 (hardcover : alk. paper) -- ISBN 1-932559-87-6 (ado-
      be ebook : alk. paper) 1. Latini, Brunetto, 1220-1295.
      2. Latini, Brunetto, 1220-1295--Influence. 3. Authors,
      Italian--To 1500--Biography. 4. Dante Alighieri, 1265-
      1321. I. Title.
  PQ4473.K64 2006
  808'.0092--dc22

                                            2006007746

Illumination 8, "Column from Latini's tomb" © 2005 by
  Matthew Blakesley. Used by permission.
Cover design by David Blakesley
Printed on acid-free paper.

Parlor Press, LLC is an independent publisher of scholarly and trade titles in print and multimedia formats. This book is available in paper, cloth and Adobe eBook formats from Parlor Press on the World Wide Web at http://www.parlorpress.com or through online and brick-and mortar bookstores. For submission information or to find out about Parlor Press publications, write to Parlor Press, 816 Robinson St., West Lafayette, Indiana, 47906, or e-mail editor@parlorpress.com.

For the most important women in my life:

My loving mother and mentor—*Elaine Mullins Kleine*
My wonderful sister and lifelong friend—
Patricia Rumbaugh
My beloved daughter, now my guide—*Amy Kleine*
My dear wife and partner—*Susan Martin Kleine*
My mother-in-law and second mother—
Isabel Martin Waggoner

Contents

Acknowledgments   xi
Introduction   3
    The Genesis of a Pilgrimage   3
    Toward a Motive and a Map   8

PART I: IN SEARCH OF ANSWERS AMONG THE BOOKS   15

1 Brunetto Latini, Notary and Writer   17
    Pre-Exile Praxis—Brunetto and the Brown Ink of Civic Writing   21
    Post-Exile Writing—Latini and the Dark Ink of Literary Posterity   26

2 Latini, Teacher of Dante, By His Student Damned   39
    The First Path—Latini's Teaching of Dante   46
    The Second Path—Dante's Damnation of His Teacher   52
    The Third Path—Material/Historical Transcendence of the "Treasure"   60

3 The Currency of Latini's Rhetorical Treasure   65
    Latini's Vernacularization and Application of Cicero   71

CONTENTS

Latini's Contributions to the Ars Dictaminis and the
  Rhetoric of Writing 80
A Rhetorician for the Here and Now 86

PART II: TOWARD AN OPEN BOOK OF MY OWN 91

4 On Foot in Florence 93

5 The Illuminating Presence of Julia
 Bolton Holloway 108
  Julia's Story 112
  Latini's Obscurity and the Revival of Interest in
   Him 114
  Latini and Orality 115
  Latini and Literacy 116
  Latini as Rhetorician 117
  Latini and the Canon of Arrangement 118
  Latini and a Curriculum for Ethical and Mediatory
   Applications of Rhetoric 119

6 Homecoming and an Open Book 123

 Works Cited 131
 Index 133
 About the Author 141

Illuminations

Albero 1: Dante's organization of the
　　Seventh Circle of Hell.　*56*

Albero 2: Medieval conception of the guidance
　　and control of the Human Being.　*57*

Illumination 1: A stony trace of the past.　*94*

Illumination 2: A street poem for peace.　*96*

Illumination 3: Graffiti in the *Sottopassaggio*.　*98*

Illumination 4: *Sottopassaggio* graffiti aimed
　　at speakers of English.　*99*

Illumination 5: Michelangelo's caricature of Savaronola?　*100*

Illumination 6: Bust of Cicero.　*101*

Illumination 7: Column from Latini's tomb,
　　an obscure memorial.　*102*

Illumination 8: Statue of Dante, next
　　to Santa Croce.　*103*

Illumination 9: Santa Maggiore, literal place
　　of Latini's "burial."　*104*

Illumination 10: Off the beaten track, on
　　the Via Brunetto Latini.　*105*

Illumination 11: Peace banner on the Via
　　Brunetto Latini.　*106*

Illumination 12: Banner urging for no more war
　　on the Via Brunetto Latini.　*107*

Illuminations

Illumination 13: Gatehouse of the English Cemetery.   *108*

Illumination 14: Julia Holloway with a copy of Latini's Book.   *113*

Illumination 15: Julia Holloway, a medievalist for the twenty-first century.   *121*

Acknowledgments

As he travels from *Inferno* to *Paradiso*, Dante acknowledges guidance from both Virgil and Beatrice. In my own pilgrimage, my search for Dante's teacher, Brunetto Latini, I have enjoyed the guidance, especially, of my daughter, Amy Kleine, and the medievalist and Latini scholar, Julia Bolton Holloway. In Florence, it was my daughter's introduction to Massimiliano Chiamenti, a Dante scholar and rock musician, that led to my initial interest in Brunetto Latini. Throughout my search, Amy has been an invaluable resource, reader, and guide, helping me to understand better the Italian history and culture in which Latini needs to be situated. My reading of Julia Holloway's important scholarship regarding Latini, and also her marvelous translation of Latini's pilgrimage poem, were foundational to my understanding of Latini's significance as a rhetorician and teacher. And Julia's collaborative spirit, evinced in both her emails to me and her conversation with me in Florence, led me to the realization that my "Book" is as much about her work and influence as it is about Latini's.

My wife, Susan, also served as a guide, providing patient reading of rough drafts and invaluable feedback as I struggled to find my way as a writer. And my uncle, Robert Kleine, a fellow pilgrim and friend, inspired me with his own journey through the hell of the Battle of the Bulge and his compelling written account of that difficult and heroic journey.

Michael Kleine

My former student, Matthew Abraham, who did his doctoral work at Purdue University and is now with the Department of English at DePaul, has become my teacher in matters having to do with critical theory and the rhetoric of resistance. His friendship and guidance have been ongoing—and formative to my recent scholarship, writing, and teaching.

David Blakesley, my Parlor Press editor, provided invaluable assistance and guidance as *Searching for Latini* neared publication. He is the best kind of editor: patient, supportive, critically astute, and always available.

In addition, I owe thanks to colleagues (and guides) from several disciplines outside of my own here at the University of Arkansas at Little Rock, who listened to me as I babbled on and on about Latini, or who read my work as I wrote and revised: Thomas Kaiser and Stephen Recken of the Department of History; Allan Ward, retired now from the Department of Speech Communication; Robert Boury, of the Department of Music; and Clara Jane Rubarth, now with the Department of English at the University of Arkansas at Fort Smith. I owe special thanks to Laura Smoller, a medievalist with the Department of History who knew about Latini long before I did; Michelle Fontaine, formerly an Italian historian with the Department of History; Carol Thompson of the Department of Speech Communication, who read and commented on my manuscript in its entirety; and James Levernier, of the Department of English, who traveled with me in Italy, shared my growing enthusiasm over Latini, and provided invaluable insights and bibliographical assistance.

In my own department, the Department of Rhetoric and Writing, I owe thanks to those who provided support and guidance at key points in my search, despite my figurative "exile": Richard Raymond, my Chair when I began my search, now Chair of the Department of English at Mississippi State University; Charles Anderson; Suzann Barr; Earnest Cox; Huey Crisp; Sally Crisp; and Toran Isom. I owe special thanks to George Jensen, current Chair of my department, who read and commented on my manuscript in its entirety, and to Andrea Herrmann, who helped me discover the point and purpose of *Searching for Latini*.

Also in my department, I wish to thank Larry Henthorn for his invaluable technological guidance.

Finally, I owe thanks to my students in a special-topics course on Cicero and Latini that I taught last summer: Jay Arrowood, Joseph Guellich, Michael Hodge, Nathan Larson, Esther Mahnken, Todd Mills, and Iresa Subblefield. More like colleagues than students, they read a draft version of *Searching for Latini*, provided helpful feedback, and encouraged me to seek publication. I owe special thanks to Susan Walker, who sat in on that class, and who has read and responded to my writing for many years now. Her critical insights have significantly guided my writing.

Searching for Latini

Introduction

THE GENESIS OF A PILGRIMAGE

> When I had journeyed half of our life's way,
> I found myself within a shadowed forest,
> for I had lost the path that does not stray.
>
> —Dante, *The Inferno*

"Who would you say is the most important Italian rhetorician other than those who, like Cicero, spoke and wrote in Latin? Is there one who especially would have influenced Dante?" My daughter, Amy, and her friend, Massimiliano Chiamenti, a Dante scholar and rock musician, were chatting with me in a little coffee bar near the Piazza Savonarola in Florence. The day before, I had taken a train up the Arno to Arezzo to see the statue of Petrarch there. My daughter had arranged the meeting with "Max," as he asked to be called, so that I could learn more about Dante and map out short trips to take during the ensuing days. She has lived and worked in Florence for the last fifteen years, and during my visits to see her, I spend the time while she is at work searching for places in Tuscany that are haunted by the ghosts of medieval and Renaissance writers or artists. My daughter has taught me a little Italian, but I am barely functional ("cave-man level," Amy laughs), and Max had taken pity on me, shifting from Italian to English as the conversation turned to Dante and then to the question I asked.

Without much of a pause, Max answered, "That's easy. Brunetto Latini."

"Who was he? I've never heard of him." (I asked the question with some embarrassment since Max knows I am a teacher of rhetoric and writing in America.)

"Oh," enthused Max, "he was Dante's teacher! Like Dante, he wrote in the vernacular, in the true Italian, and also"—Max looked pained—"in French."

In the past I had visited many places in Tuscany having to do with or clearly memorializing Dante in various ways—the Ponte Vecchio, his statue beside Santa Croce, his house, plaques marking places mentioned in *The Divine Comedy*. I was interested in seeing more Dante memorials (there are over thirty plaques I have been told), but Max's response to my question suggested a new historical figure on whom I might focus. So I asked Max, "Where might I go to see something having to do with Latini?"

Max frowned: "There is not much that has to do with Latini. You might go see Santa Maria Maggiore, where he is buried, but otherwise there is very little to see. Dante put his teacher in hell, you know. And ever since [. . .]"

That afternoon, after making a number of wrong turns in the labyrinth of Florence's streets, and after inquiring several times for directions without luck, I finally bumbled my way to Santa Maria Maggiore, a relatively obscure Gothic church, one of the city's oldest, built in the eleventh century and rebuilt in the thirteenth century. There I was able to see the symbolic marker of Latini's tomb, a marble column that, as far as I knew at the time, was the single Florentine memorial to the teacher of Dante. Later, I was to learn just how appropriate the memorial is, given Latini's association of a secure column and an unstagnant fountain with the style of his own mentor in matters of rhetoric, Cicero.

Introduction

Somewhere over the Atlantic, on my return flight to the United States, I began to reflect on my life as a teacher of writing. Like most teachers of writers, I am obscure. And like many teachers of writing, it is the writing my students produce that matters most to me. But why would a great rhetorician and the teacher of Dante be consigned to such obscurity? We know very little, of course, about whoever it was who taught rhetoric to Shakespeare, even though his work reflects considerable understanding of classical rhetoric. But why would someone who was known to teach a writer with the stature of Dante be so under memorialized? After all, Latini's translations of Aristotle and Cicero, his poetry, and his writing about rhetoric still survive. And why, as I was to discover, do American rhetoricians know little or nothing about the rhetorician who, according to Max, was not only Dante's teacher, but also a significant influence on the persuasive and literary discourse of Florence, the political and intellectual flower of the Renaissance?

In my journey more than halfway through my life as a teacher of writing and rhetoric, I was clearly in the shadows, not only as a teacher, but also as a scholar—as someone who should have known about the great significance of another teacher, one who had lived and worked in the thirteenth century and who had been unfairly condemned to relative obscurity. This shadowy teacher had influenced Dante, but who, exactly, was he? And what is the contemporary significance of his historical legacy? Even though I was heading home, I knew, then, that I was on a new path, the beginning of a pilgrimage in which I would search for Latini. I needed a guide.

༃

My intention to search for and write about Latini from the persona of a pilgrim was motivated, in part, by the intertextual pull of Dante's great allegorical pilgrimage, *The*

Michael Kleine

Divine Comedy. After returning from Florence and my brief introduction to Latini (this was several years ago), I began to reread Dante's tale of his journey from Inferno to Paradise, finding along the way Canto XV of *The Inferno,* in which Dante, guided by Virgil, finds his mentor in the Seventh Circle of Hell, among the sodomites. I decided, after this brief glimpse of Latini's damnation, that I would attempt to go on a pilgrimage of my own. As a teacher, inevitably sympathetic to other teachers, I hoped to find Latini in a place other than hell, not damned, but merely obscured. I would later discover the profound connection between exile and pilgrimage, for both Latini and Dante, but in the beginning, I hoped only to search for Latini—first in any available literature and then experientially during my next visit to Florence. I certainly did not plan to suffer any sort of alienation or exile from my home country or from my work as an American teacher of rhetoric and writing.

But I wondered, at the outset of my journey, what was required of a pilgrim? In the family stories my mother told me as a boy, our roots on her side of the family (her maiden name was Mullins) went back to Priscilla Mullins and the Mayflower. Wasn't I a descendant of pilgrims? If so, why was I relatively clueless about what it meant, historically, to be a pilgrim, and why was I about to embark on a pilgrimage that would take me not west, to the New World, but east to Italy and back to a time before the New World had been discovered, at least in American mythology, by Columbus, himself an Italian? My mother might have served as a kind of guide in this pilgrimage business, as a Beatrice, perhaps, but she died a little over six years ago. And so, groping, I did a number of Internet searches, hoping to find a site or a book or a scholar that might help me learn more about Latini, might help me understand the nuances of thinking and acting like a pilgrim . The searches, especially those using "Latini" as the key word, led me primar-

Introduction

ily to a living scholar, Julia Bolton Holloway, who is now the curator of the English Cemetery in Florence. I became especially interested in Holloway and her work when a link led me to a particular book, based on her doctoral dissertation, entitled *The Pilgrim and the Book: A Study of Dante, Langland, and Chaucer*.

At the beginning of *The Pilgrim and the Book* (the "Genesis," as she might call it, echoing Frank Kermode), Holloway explains the antiquity and complexity of the "figure of the pilgrim," who "whether medieval or Renaissance, stood at a joining of roads: on the one hand lay a Hellenic past, on the other a Hebraic one." She adds, "These two traditions, though opposed to each other, were reconciled in the concept of the 'Exile,' the 'Pilgrim,' which yoked their contrary modes into one being. In flesh and blood, the figure of Everyman as pilgrim acted out the words of Books, of the Odyssey and the Bible" (1). Holloways capitalization of "Book" and "Books" is telling: in so doing, she suggests not only the unity of *the* Book (as opposed to a chapter) but also its great allegorical potential. As the "Apocalypse" of Holloway's Book nears, she asks this interesting question about medieval pilgrimage poems in particular: "Why is the figure of the poet present in these poems and as a pilgrim?" She notes that "the figures of the poets are present in their poems, the creators within their creations, in their own image" and that "the other characters in their poems are as if fragmentations of themselves" (209).

After rereading *The Divine Comedy* and Holloway's Book, more questions than answers started to occur to me regarding my own forthcoming pilgrimage. Although I would most certainly figure as The Pilgrim in my own rendering of my journey, would a relatively secular and non-allegorical search count as a true pilgrimage? And if I were not, in fact, exiled, but instead engaged in a search for an exiled rhetorician and teacher, could I trope myself as a pilgrim? But a sense of my identity as a Mullins kept nudging at me, urging me to see my search for Latini as one that had more significance than a tourist's trip. After all, the aim of my search would be to understand not only Latini's obscurity as a teacher of writing, but also my own obscurity and the obscurity of all of us who aspire not to be great, but to teach great writers. Perhaps, after all, I was the "Everyperson," the "Everyteacher," who has searched to understand his or her own identity as a sort of midwife, as the helper of the one who is known as an author, who gives birth to persuasive and important texts. And most certainly, like Dante, I was in need of guides who might help me find my way.

I determined to push aside the questions concerning my status as pilgrim, and to begin the journey. I would start by reading the Books, the work written by Latini and by those who, like Holloway, have written about his writing—and then, carrying as a staff the writing of others, I would, bearded and pilgrim-like, return physically to the place where Latini lived and worked. Like Dante, I would journey from one realm to another, from reading to experience, and, perhaps, I would find transcendence of my ignorance, find, even, exile from my world of shadows.

Toward a Motive and a Map

Before I go much further with this pilgrim tale, I will take a little space, for myself and for any readers I might have in the future, to get oriented, to "justify" my motives (in the Miltonic sense of typographical justification) and then to map where I have been and where I am going. Such orientation and mapping must begin with me, with where I find myself in terms of what I have been reading and thinking since returning from my last trip to Florence. I am not much of a poet, but like Dante, I am "creator within my own creation." What does such a state of being mean? This

INTRODUCTION

is a difficult question to answer. To locate myself as a creator within my own creation, within the text I am in the process of writing even now, is to understand that my journey as writer is just beginning. Thus, I find myself already a pilgrim within the "Book," at the Genesis of the text I now inhabit and will continue to inhabit for some time. In terms of my search for Latini, however, a search that so far has been, in a literal sense, among texts outside of my own text, I find myself at a half-way point. I have traveled from text to text as a reader, roaming from Dante's Book to Latini's Books to Holloway's Books and to the Books and articles written by other scholars of Latini. It is telling, I think, that my journey as a reader has not been without travel and a sense of exile: although I have not yet left my physical station here in Arkansas, I have had to rely heavily on the Internet and on interlibrary loan in order to get anywhere at all. In short, I have had to rely on moving outward, electronically and textually, from the library of my home university, the University of Arkansas at Little Rock. The journals in my home discipline, rhetoric and writing, have been of little help, for they have little or nothing to say about Latini. In a sense, then, I find myself exiled from both my home library and my home discipline.

Why do I need to reflect upon such an exile at all? The answer to this question has much to do with what Kenneth Burke would call "motive," and also with "identification." It seems fitting to me that I interrogate my own intellectual and pedagogical exile as I attempt to become more or less "consubstantial" with Latini, who was himself an exiled teacher when he wrote his great encyclopedia and treatise on rhetoric in France (and in French), *Li Livres dou Tresor*. My pilgrim motive emerges from a growing sense that the textual search for Latini already has involved traveling away from the American rhetorical canon, from my home discipline.

Although I have already found something of the ghost of Latini by moving outward from the version of rhetorical history that is usually taught in American universities, he is missing, utterly, in the texts and documents with which I am familiar and that I have taught in the past. The irony of this is perplexing: I am beginning to understand that, even though Latini is in exile from the discourse of those of us who teach rhetoric and writing in our pilgrim country at the beginning of the twenty-first century, he may well be one of the most important influences on our understanding of the great republican rhetor and rhetorician, Cicero, on our sense of the importance and shape of public forensic and deliberative writing, on the way we teach students to write not only academic papers, but also letters, and on the way we teach the construction of ethos in relationship to persuasive writing. Indeed, Latini's work may well be indirectly and intertextually a shaper of our Constitution. That central document, which is at the heart of our nation's deliberative and forensic practice, is most certainly a brilliant text, but it is not entirely original as a genre, a speech act, or a text; it may in fact be deeply indebted to Latini's important lead in writing and enacting documents that, in both function and form, enable polities to govern themselves and to establish the rights of all citizens. For it was Latini, not Dante (especially in medieval and pre-Renaissance Florence), who, as an influential member of the Guelf party, opposed the notion of empire (and of an emperor), and who attempted to promote the kind of discourse that informs and enables democratic praxis.

My aim, therefore, is not to claim authority as a scholar of Latini. It is, instead, to roam outward among the important texts written by scholars like Holloway in an effort to find Latini, and then to bring him back to America, where he might be given his due by those of us who are interested in the history of rhetoric and the teaching of writ-

Introduction

ing. For some reason the movie *Field of Dreams* comes to mind: my pilgrim aim is to search for Latini across time, and then take him to the living baseball game of the American canon of rhetoric, where his historical pain, inflicted by Dante's damnation and intensified by his obscurity, might be "eased."

But here I must also confess a more personal aim. I am a teacher of writing, mainly, and as a teacher I have resigned myself to the obscurity in which most teachers, perhaps especially teachers of writing, find themselves. I accept this obscurity, hoping like many teachers of writing that it is my students who will emerge, through their writing, as important, as memorable. As a writing teacher, though, I deeply feel the obscurity of all other writing teachers, and I believe that some of them—especially the one who taught Dante and who was himself a significant writer—deserve to be exhumed from obscurity, deserve to be memorialized by something more than a column of a tomb hidden away in Santa Maria Maggiore.

My personal and public aims were reinforced by an email message that Holloway sent me after I wrote her to request an interview during my anticipated return to Florence, where she now resides. Reflecting on Latini's obscurity, she wrote to me that Latini *"Deserves* to be better known and shared more" (my emphasis). Although she is from England originally, Holloway has taught both at the University of Colorado and Princeton University, and she explained to me: "I think American rhetoricians don't know his work because these texts" (Latini's written legacy) "are neither accessible nor in English." Holloway has already worked hard both to translate Latini's work and to underscore and explain its significance, but she invited me to collaborate in this work, adding, "That's the kind of scholarship I prefer, where everybody gets ahead and shares with each other, so much more being learned and taught in the process." Nowhere near the scholar that Holloway is, I felt honored to be invited to join her in her project. And her invitation has helped me clarify my aim, to understand, better, my role as a pilgrim: it is to write as an American teacher, and an obscure one at that, in order to better understand what Latini might teach me and to *share* Holloway's work (and the work of other Latini scholars) with American rhetoricians and teachers of writing.

As I begin to write in an effort to share, I know that in Holloway I have found a magnificent guide. So, yes, I might reside in this, my own Book, as a guided pilgrim. And like Dante, whose *Divine Comedy* provides maps of the landscapes of the Inferno, Purgatory, and Paradise, I will endeavor to articulate a map of my Book. Really, I will endeavor to provide a hierarchical list of the parts of the landscapes I plan to traverse, believing that Latini himself, a great cataloger, would approve.

My Book will first relate what I have learned by reading, by traveling in the Books of others. It will include translated passages from Latini's Books, and it will endeavor to answer the following questions:

1. Who, exactly, was Brunetto Latini, and in what sort of historical context was he situated? What did he do (as notary, ambassador, political leader, and teacher), and what did he write as both rhetorician and poet?

2. Why would a clearly successful student, Dante, consign his teacher, Latini, to hell? Why does Dante decide to damn Latini, the man, but not his most important rhetorical treatise, whose scattered pages appear as a treasure in Paradise? What, exactly, did Latini teach to Dante?

3. How has Latini's work been treated historically, and why do American teachers of rhetoric and writing know so little about him? What *has* Latini taught,

albeit indirectly, to those of us who teach rhetoric and writing? Why *should* American writing teachers, insofar as they are concerned with the history and practice of rhetoric, learn from Latini?

The second part of my Book will be more travel narrative than literature review. In it, I plan to tell of a return journey to Florence. If all goes as planned, I will interweave the following:

- Journal entries concerning my trip
- An account of my return to Santa Maria Maggiore
- Photographs of the streets and places Latini would have frequented
- An interview with my daughter, who studied Dante at the University of Florence
- Most importantly, an interview with Julia Bolton Holloway

Finally, the "Apocalypse" of my Book will suggest that there should be no Apocalypse for the sharing of work regarding Brunetto Latini. It will provide a final personal reflection on Latini's great significance (and on the particular contributions of Julia Bolton Holloway to understanding that significance), and it will suggest ways other American rhetoricians and teachers might search for, find, and apply Latini's work, a "little treasure" that, by no means, should be buried in obscurity. By concluding with a more or less personal bibliography, I hope to suggest that with the close of my own Book (so indebted to the work of medievalists and archival scholars), other Books, important Books, might be opened by those of us who care deeply about the teaching of rhetoric and writing. If all goes well, the Apocalypse will in fact be a Genesis.

Michael Kleine

Part I: In Search of Answers Among the Books

1 Brunetto Latini, Notary and Writer

Anyone who has traveled extensively in Italy knows that, even today, it is the city, not the nation, that is at the heart of an Italian's political, linguistic, and cultural identity. In Florence, for instance, people will tell you that they speak the "true Italian," that their dialect is the one in which the great Dante wrote. Moreover, they will tell you that Florentine cuisine is the best in all Italy; that the artistic, literary, and intellectual history of Florence is richer and more important than, say, the artistic, literary, and intellectual history of Siena (or even Rome), having produced, among others, Michelangelo, Botticelli, Petrarch, Boccaccio, and Galileo Galilei; that the local soccer team has the finest, albeit not always the most successful, soccer players in Italy; that Florentine culture in general is far superior to the culture of other Italian cities, especially those cities south of Rome; and that "Firenze" (which means "little flower") was the birthplace of the Renaissance. People in Florence believe that their Duomo is the greatest architectural wonder of Italy, perhaps of the world. And they believe that it is their city, the home of the Medici family and also the home of Machiavelli, that most profoundly shaped Italian notions of beneficent government and pragmatic political practice. The people of Florence will also tell you that their city, above all cities in Italy, created a city state modeled directly on the classical democratic values enacted by both the

Athenians and the Roman Republic. Indeed, the people of Florence are more likely to compare themselves in a superlative way with residents of other Italian cities than they are with residents of other nations. This kind of city-centered pride and identity can be felt across all of Italy. Indeed, it is a pride and identity that can be traced back to the Italian city states that emerged before the Renaissance.

In answering the question, Who, exactly, was Brunetto Latini? a good starting point might be, quite simply, that he was a citizen of the *comune* of Florence in the thirteenth century ("citizen" being a far better word than "resident" and "comune," implying community, a better word than "commune," with its ideological overtones), even though he spent part of his life in exile from his home city. To this it is important to add that Latini was a committed member of the Guelf party, a republican political party that defined itself in relationship to Florence and in opposition to Siena, its arch enemy and the heart of Ghibelline commitment to empire and the governance of an emperor.

I write all of the above with a sense that I may be oversimplifying the Italian political landscape of the thirteenth century, but with the conviction that, whether we consider Latini as a rhetorician, a teacher, an ambassador, a notary, a translator of key classical texts, or a poet, in all of his roles he was a politically and ideologically committed representative of Florentine republican values and, like Cicero, a staunch opponent of hierarchically static and imperially constituted forms of government. This having been said, I will rely personally on Holloway's guidance in my search to find and portray two aspects of Latini's life as a writer—a life that begins with his writing in both Latin and Italian, with his professional praxis as a notary and diplomat, but that culminates in his writing in the vernacular of important literary and rhetorical texts. These culminating texts, I believe, are of special significance to those of us who teach rhetoric and writing in America. They include pioneering translations of classical Greek and Roman rhetorical texts into a vernacular language, such as *La Rettorica,* his translation of Cicero's *De Inventione;* the writing in Italian of an allegorical pilgrimage poem, *Il Tesoretto,* that has considerable implications for the study of rhetorically situated allegory (and that most clearly influenced Dante); and his monumental advancement of rhetorical theory in the *lingua franca* of his day (vernacular French), the third part of *Li Livres dou Tresor.* Especially, I will rely on Holloway's *Twice-Told Tales,* her brilliant characterizing of the palimpsesting, the "double writing," that is at the heart of the corpus of Latini's writing. Holloway's own careful scholarship, it must be noted, discovers Latini in the Florentine histories of Filippo and Giovanni Villani, among others, and in primary Latini documents that can be found in archives in Florence, the Vatican, and even England.

However, it is on a personal, somewhat whimsical note that I will begin my characterization, noticing at the outset Latini's first name and his naming of his children, for it is in the naming of ourselves and others that we often reveal much about what we believe and value. Holloway tells us that Brunetto Latini's birth date is uncertain, but that thanks to civic documents we know that his daughter, Bianca, was married in 1248. The naming of a daughter, for me, has great significance: my own daughter (now my teacher and collaborator in matters involving the Italian language and Italian culture) was named "Amy" with the hope that she would someday understand how truly beloved she was and is. Several months ago, my wife and I took home a new Pomeranian puppy. My wife, upon selecting an unusual Pom, which was white in color, agreed to give me naming rights. I chose the name Bianca—meaning "white" in Italian—not only because of an impulse to honor the language that my daughter loves, but also to remember Latini, who was at that point looming larger and larger in my life as a rhetorician and teacher of writing.

We also know that Latini had two sons, one of whom was named Perseo. I focus here on Bianca and Perseo, especially, because these two names, along with Brunetto's own name, evoke cloths and colors often associated with notions of textuality, and these were surely possible associations for Latini: Bianca, meaning "white," may have suggested the parchment upon which texts were written; in contrast Perseo, meaning "dark purple," suggests the ink in which literary and philosophical texts were written. Brunetto's own name, meaning "brown," suggests the particular ink associated with chancery documents. It is impossible to know if Latini deliberately named Bianca and Perseo to suggest the literary kinship of the white page with the ink written upon it—or to suggest that Latini saw in his children's names a metaphor for the birth of textual potential and perhaps, even, transcendence of his use of brown ink in his work as a notary. However, Holloway shows us, in her portrayal of Latini, that he was a writer prone to puns and intertextual allusions, as were other medieval writers, including Dante. Focusing on Dante's puns at the beginning of her Book, *Twice-Told Tales,* she writes: "In Dante's *Inferno XIII,* we meet a figure mirroring Brunetto Latino of *Inferno XV.* In a scene of terror Dante plucks a dead twig which then bleeds—one can add that it bleeds brown chancery ink—*Da che fatto fu poi di sangue bruno.* [. . .] Later Dante will gather up further fallen leaves, folia, restoring them to an unnamed Florentine suicide" (1).

As a teacher of writing, I want to think of Latini mainly in terms of the documents and texts that he wrote. In other words, for me, Latini was (and is) what he wrote. His own identity, of course, was deeply grounded in his praxis as a writer of chancery documents and of politically motivated letters. And so it is Brunetto, the user of brown ink, a notary, a Chancellor, and a political citizen of Florence who, in my opinion, must be considered first, before he is, in the end, figured as Latini, father of Bianca and Perseo, a vernacular poet, a translator of Aristotle and Cicero, and the author of an overlooked, but clearly important, rhetorical treatise (and treasure). Perhaps Latini himself would approve of such a characterization and order, for, as Holloway argues, "It was Brunetto's nature to use praxis first, then to draw theories from that praxis" (262).

Pre-Exile Praxis—Brunetto and the Brown Ink of Civic Writing

As Brunetto was returning from an embassy to Spain in 1260, he learned in the Pass of Roncevalles that he had been exiled. The Florentine Guelfs had just been defeated in the disastrous Battle of Montaperti by Manfred, son of Fredrick II, and the Sienese Ghibellines. As a result, Florence's communal government, the *Primo Popolo* (which arose in the middle of the thirteenth century when Florence rebelled against its land-owning aristocracy), was forced to go underground. That Guelf government had been deeply influenced by the Republic of Rome; it was guided by its *Anziani*, or Senate, and its *podesta*, an outsider elected to govern as fairly as possible, relatively free of factional or self interest. Brunetto had played an important role in Florence's experiment with republican democracy, serving as a diplomat and notary.

It was in his role as notary and statesman that Brunetto composed important documents, treaties, and letters. In thirteenth-century Italy, the position of notary was an important one, connected as it was to the legal work of the chancery. Holloway explains in *Twice-Told Tales* that Americans might not understand the importance of the professional notary: "That profession in Europe to this day is of the greatest importance, though not in America, enabling records to be kept in perpetuity in accordance with imperial Roman law and requiring a great knowledge of the Roman Empire's language and customs" (169). Indeed, Brunetto's professional writing, before and after his exile, was included in the *Epistolarium,* a compilation of letters of state that was initiated by Pier delle Vigne, the Ghibelline Chancellor to Fredrick II, as a means of guiding and instructing subsequent chancery officials. However, Brunetto's written documents were not merely included in the *Epistolarium* and the Ghibelline tradition of imperial authority; indeed, they resisted and changed that discursive tradition, including in the *Epistolarium* not only texts written in Latin, but also translations from speeches that had been made in the context of the Roman Republic during the time of Catilina's treason and Cicero's great orations. Although imperial chanceries remained powerful during Brunetto's lifetime, Brunetto and other Guelfs endeavored to, in Holloway's words, "vernacularize them." Holloway underscores the importance of Brunetto's resistance to Pier delle Vigne's chancery and his compilation of documents written in Latin: "While the actual letters of state were written in notarial and chancery Latin, and are given, in some versions of the *Epistolarium,* in their original Latin, these collections generally take pride in presenting themselves in the liberating Italian vernacular so that they might be immediately comprehensible to their readers" and so that they might be used "for teaching purposes" (199).

Brunetto, then, wrote to resist a dominant chancery discourse (the discourse of civil-law courts of equity) and to participate in what Paulo Freire might call a "liberatory pedagogy," one aimed at providing to vernacular speakers participatory access to the "bank" of chancery documents. Thus, contemporary compositionists might look to Brunetto's praxis of literacy as ideologically situated, as a great historical instance of writing's role as a liberating and democratizing technology, available to ordinary people who have been oppressed by elite, exclusionary discourses of power and control. Indeed, the kind of vernacular literacy promoted by Brunetto, and also by his student, Dante, was at the heart of Florentine and Guelf ideology and political practice. Commenting on Brunetto's significance as a practicing notary and Florentine official, Holloway writes: "Brunetto was not the original writer that Dante was. He was, instead, the great translator, the '*vulgarizzatore*' of the past so that it could shape the present and the future" (206). Indeed, Brunetto's "liberatory" documents might be best understood as contributions not so much to "literature," but to a literacy that enabled democratic values and political practice to thrive. Writing about the key role that literacy played in Florentine discourse and Guelf political life, Holloway stresses: "In the archives for the Guelf periods of government one sees the monuments, the *capitoli*, the *pergamene* scrolls, the *protocolli* which indicate an intense use of writing and speaking, decision making and record keeping. When the Ghibellines were in power such documents were in little evidence" (206). She adds, focusing on Brunetto's participation in Florentine vernacular and reflective literacy:

> The ancient texts were made accessible and immediate, teaching their young Florentine readers, equating and translating as they did a Jerusalem, an Athens and a Rome, for their readers so they could, thereby, learn to reflect and mirror them, likewise achieving their greatness, their great energy. He provided for them *copia,* both copy and abundance, for them in turn to manipulate to their ends. (206)

Many of Brunetto's legal documents might be understood as public, relatively accessible speech acts, declaring as they did agreements that affected deeply the life and politics of the Florentine people. They were "read out in a loud voice to the assembled comune, summoned to such places as Santa Reparta or San Lorenzo or the Badia by the ringing of church bells, and the documents were thus signed and witnessed publicly as legal, political *acta,* speech acts, words made into deeds" (*Twice-Told Tales,* 6). But Brunetto's practical documents, along with his later literary and rhetorical texts, also served as teaching documents, helping to promote ongoing literacy of a decidedly critical nature. The documents "could be remembered well by the assembled citizens who heard their phrases," but "they would be even better remembered by young men Latini could have taught by having them copy out into the *Capitoli* the various *Acta* of the Comune, into the *Epistolarium* the various letters of state between popes and emperors, into the *Tesoro* texts of Aristotle and Cicero, and perhaps the even more subversive accounts of the plotting of the Sicilian Vespers in the later *Tesoro* manuscripts" (*Twice-Told Tales,* 6).

In contemporary terms, then, Brunetto's professional writing praxis contributed directly to a literacy that was public, participatory, and even liberatory. In "Chancery and Comedy: Brunetto Latini and Dante Alighieri" (an article in a web journal, *Lectura Dantis,* written as a brief version of what was to grow into *Twice-Told Tales*), Holloway provides a succinct and helpful survey of Latini's professional/political writing, focusing on seven extant practical documents that were clearly written by Latini, as well as others that he probably wrote. These documents were written both before and after Latini's exile, in both Latin and Italian, but I will mention only two that were written before his exile, hoping to suggest the genesis of his practical writing and also its linguistic, rhetorical, and generic range.

Brunetto Latini, Notary and Writer

The first document, a peace treaty written in Latin in 1254, might be viewed by new rhetoricians, interested in cooperative applications of persuasive discourse as an instance of negotiatory writing. The document, twice-signed by feuding Florentine Guelfs and Sienese Ghibellines, served as the basis for a temporary peace—even though underground plotting led to the Battle of Montaperti in 1260, Florence's defeat at the hands of King Manfred of Sicily and the Sienese, and Brunetto's own exile. In "Chancery and Comedy," Holloway informs us that the document was signed and witnessed by the Florentines at the Church of Santa Reparta (*"ad sonum campanarum comunis,* to the sound of the bells of the *Comune,* in the presence of the Anziani, the Senate, and all other officials of the *Comune* and people of Florence"). The Sienese later signed the document at Montereggione. Holloway notes, "The document in question is today still in Siena, written in Brunetto Latini's clear and lovely hand, signed with his notarial sign of a lilied column," the column being, of course, emblematic of Brunetto's intertextual and personal linkage with Cicero, and a foreshadowing of the column that even today mark's Brunetto's tomb in Santa Maria Maggiore.

The second pre-exile document, probably authored by Brunetto shortly before the Battle of Montaperti in 1260, represents an interesting rhetorical turn away from Brunetto's notarial involvement in the writing of peace treaties— negotiatory work that was to continue throughout his life. It is a letter sent by Florence to the *comune* of Pavia, mocking Pavian Ghibellines for their outrage over the death of the Abbot Tesauro of Vallombrosa, who, suspected of conspiring with the Ghibellines, was murdered in Florence, his head torn off by an angry mob. Agonistically toned and decidedly sarcastic, perhaps even sacrilegious, the letter provides a window into Brunetto's resistance of received chancery discourse, and also to the intertextual punning that was typical of not only Pier delle Vigne, but also Brunetto himself—and, later, Dante. Indeed, Brunetto's pun on the Abbot's name, "Tesauro"—meaning, roughly, "treasure"—will emerge again in the Italian title of his allegorical poem, *Il Tesoretto,* and in the French title of his encyclopedia/rhetoric, *Li Livres dou Tresor.*" The pun will later help explain Dante's treatment of Latini's "Book" in *The Divine Comedy.*

The rhetorical complexity of the letter to the Pavian Ghibellines is remarkable, using, as it does, not the Ciceronian style favored by Brunetto and Florentine Guelfs, but the Ghibelline imperial-chancery style of Pier delle Vigne, characterized by deliberate Biblical punning. (Pier delle Vigne had punned upon his own name, and in so doing he had suggested that he, like Christ, was the "true Vine.") Holloway explains that, in the letter, "Pavians are told not to lay up their 'treasure' on earth' (punning on the Abbot's name, 'Tesauro,') 'but in heaven,' basing the text for this sermon about murder on Matthew 29:16–24." In other words, Brunetto's letter confronted, through sarcasm, the stylistic proclivities and excesses of received chancery discourse. The murder of Abbot Tesauro, along with Brunetto's confrontational letter, may have served as excuse for Ghibelline aggression at Montaperti (and, ironically, indirect cause of Brunetto's own exile), but in my view the letter stands as evidence of Brunetto Latini's deep devotion to the Guelf republican cause, and also to his effort as a writer to resist and embarrass the very discursive tradition in which, as a practicing notary, he found himself.

Post-Exile Writing—Latini and the Dark Ink of Literary Posterity

I do not wish to oversimplify Latini's great contributions to the translation of classical rhetorics, to Italian literary history, and to rhetorical theory by associating them with his exile, his surname, and black (or dark-purple) ink. But it is, primarily, the writing that Latini did during his exile that lives on as Books. In my personal search for Latini, therefore, I find him in the second part of his writerly life (in what I want to call his "meta-life"), writing not only in the brown ink of his notarial profession, but also in ink that will endure in published versions of his Books, printed by presses long after his death. I now will deliberately call him Latini as I characterize his Books, aware of the irony of doing so, for the great significance of his post-exile writing is that it *was not* written in Latin. Indeed, as Holloway argues, the significance of Latini's Books lies in his effort to rhetoricize them, to write them in the vernacular, to make them accessible to citizens of his *comune,* to his students, to citizens of the world. Indeed, Latini emerges as a great rhetorician because of his commitment to what I take to be the central purpose of rhetoric—the promotion of justice and empowerment through discourse, a commitment that can be traced back to Corax of Sicily and his belief that the rhetoric and language of the law should be available to all whose lives are affected by the law.

In 1260, following the Guelf defeat at the Battle of Montaperti, Latini went into exile in France. During that exile, Latini continued to translate Aristotle and Cicero. He also wrote an extended allegorical poem, *Il Tesoretto* (in vernacular Italian), and later his encyclopedia/rhetoric, *Li Livres dou Tresor* (in vernacular French). In "A Teacher of Dante," Nathan Haskin Dole points out that Latini's exile in Paris could not have lasted very long, "for Manfred was defeated by King Charles on the last day of February, in 1265, the Ghibellines left Florence in their turn in the following November, and the Guelfs were definitely reestablished two years later, and in 1269 Brunetto Latini was *protonotario della curia* for King Charles of Sicily" (9). Dole locates Latini back home in Florence in 1273, where he resumed his professional life as "notary and secretary of councils of the Commune of Florence" and where later, in 1280, "he was one of the signatories in the famous peace between the Guelfs and Ghibellines" (9–10). He died in Florence in 1294. Nevertheless, it was in exile that Latini made his greatest contributions to the "vernacularization of rhetoric."

Holloway notes that Latini was the first vernacular translator of both Aristotle and Cicero, not only in the *Epistolarium,* but also in Latini's *La Rettorica,* a translation of *De Inventione* that was probably written during Latini's exile and that found its way, during an early stage of completion, into *Li Livres dou Tresor,* the great Book that served as a kind of textbook for future political leaders and rhetoricians. To fully understand the significance of Latini's work as a translator, one must locate his translations, as Holloway urges us to do, in relationship to his political identity as a Guelf and to the medieval tradition of reading and writing, which can best be understood by considering, as a fact and as a figure, the "palimpsest."

The political character of Latini's translations of classical rhetorical texts can be seen in how he dealt with the ideologically conservative Aristotle in contrast to the republican Cicero. Separating out the different personae adopted by Latini as he translated, Holloway writes: "One finds Brunetto Latino, when adopting the toga of Cicero, being truthful, but that when he put on the mask of Aristotle, he was devious and Machiavellian. In his persona as Aristotle he was even to deliberately mistranslate the text of the *Nicomachean Ethics* where it praised monarchy, changing this to the opposite, the praise of the comune, the republic, of government by the people, not princes" (*Twice-Told Tales,* 8). Indeed, in the *Tresor,* Latini inverted Aristotle's hierarchy of desirable forms of government—"Kingship/Aristocracy/Timocracy"—so that the third and worst became the first and best, Timocracy being, of course, a form of communal democracy. That is, "he falsified the text for communal ends" (233). Latini's faithful translation of Cicero, however, was also more than a "truthful" translation: it was writing in which he identified with the great Roman republican, even to the point of naming himself differently in *La Rettorica*. As Holloway explains, "in his Latin documents he calls himself, 'ser Brunectus Bonaccursi Latinus, notarius,'" whereas in his translation of Cicero into the vernacular "he defines both Cicero and himself as 'Rector,' as the one who taught Rhetoric, in opposition to 'Orator,' the one who used what he had been taught to speak and write well" (10–11).

Beyond their clear contribution to rhetorical history and the political vibrancy of medieval and Renaissance Florence, Latini's translations, along with *Il Tesoretto* and *Li Livres dou Tresor,* evince notions of textuality and intertextuality that seem, anachronistically, postmodern, even deconstructive. Holloway connects Latini's intertextual consciousness and writing with the notion of the palimpsest. Literally, a palimpsest is a medieval text that is written, to save parchment, on top of an earlier erased, or nearly erased, text. In terms of rhetorical motive, the palimpsest often was an effort to over-write pagan classical manuscripts with Christian narrative and doctrine. Figuratively, the palimpsest might be seen as a manifestation of an extremely sophisticated notion of the intertextual significance of writing, "new" texts being both read and written through "old texts," their meaning having to do with both past and present context. In such a way, the past was inevitably associated with the present. Thus, for Holloway, Latini's translations, indeed all of his Books, were instances of double writing, twice-told tales in which the past became a means of understanding, and rhetorically acting in, the political present. In terms familiar to contemporary American compositionists, Holloway writes, "The Middle Ages used the past as a way of thinking about their present, using that past as theory for their *praxis*" (196). Thus, in *La Rettorica,* Latini claims "that throughout the text of his translation and commentary the author was double, that he was both Cicero speaking of Rome and that he is Brunetto Latino speaking of Florence" (265), and that, in vernacular translation, "Rome, and Athens before her, were then in turn, theory to Florence's *praxis*" (207).

As palimpsests, Latini's translations were deeply intertextual, ideological, and rhetorical. And because Latini's particular political ideology was Guelf and republican, he "quarried the Latin texts of Sallust and Cicero," in particular, "vulgarizing them into Florentine Italian in order to give his readers and his students a sense of identity and the realization that Florence, like Rome, was subject to betrayal by individuals like Catilina and Farinata and to salvation by individuals like Cato, Cicero—and even Latino" (Holloway, *Twice-Told Tales,* 197).

In addition to his translations, Latini's Books, never totally original in their rich intertextuality, were also twice written, also visions of political and rhetorical possibilities for republican and democratic discourse and practice. *Il Tesoretto* (a poem in vernacular Italian) and *Li Livres dou Treso*r (an encyclopedia/rhetoric in French, the *lingua franca* of medieval Europe) give away their intertextuality with each other and with the Bible in their punning titles, which allude to the injunction in Matthew to store up treasure in heaven rather than treasure on earth. Indeed, both the *Tesoretto* and the *Tresor* are, like Latini's vernacular translations, double written, palimpsests, as they are, not only of each other, but also of other important medieval, Biblical, and classical texts. Indeed, the complicated ambages in the *Tesoretto* and the *Tresor* suggest not only how the texts might be read, but also how they might be received and applied as political and rhetorical treasures.

Brunetto Latini, Notary and Writer

Writing about the *Tesoretto* in "The Alterity and Modernity of Medieval Literature", Hans Robert Jauss points out that the modern reader may find it to be jarring, even an instance of careless didactic digressions written in doggerel, a kind of dumping of encyclopedic knowledge rather than a great narrative poem characterized by "purity of style, unity of action, judicious harmony of part and whole, unity of form and content, shape and significance" (186). Confronting what he calls the "alterity" of Latini's poem, Jauss argues for its medieval originality, intertextual though it is with what Jauss calls the "simple forms," but also deeply ironic. Indeed, as Jauss points out, Latini evokes the extant simple forms (the proverb, the fable, the exemplum, and the tale), but he employs a "totally original 'kaleidoscopic' principle of stylization, the ironic position (as opposed to the allegory of love imported from France), and the attitude of *curiositas* which announces itself for the first time as an all-encompassing motif—that new dignity of one's own questioning, for which the allegorical 'I' liberates itself and with which it crosses the threshold of the Renaissance" (186). The *Tesoretto*, then, needs to be read as an act of not only reiterating the knowledge of the day, but also resisting conventional notions of genre and power. For Jauss, a contemporary scholar and reader, it is lamentable that the *Tesoretto's* "unrecognized aesthetic precession," which medieval readers would have found not only familiar and reassuring, but also meaningful, "can obscure the historical significance as well as the poetic qualities of one of the high points of allegorical representation—indeed totally exclude it from the canon of the values of tradition" (185–86).

But by historicizing Latini's allegory—his dream vision—we can better appreciate what he was trying to say about fame and power, and also about persuasive ethos and practice. Such appreciation can begin with an understanding of the oral (and aural) qualities of the *Tesoretto*.

In *Orality and Literacy,* a Book familiar to many contemporary compositionists, Walter Ong suggests that the performance of the extended oral epic relied on the knowledge and cultural concerns of its immediate audience. Such an epic would have been less concerned with presenting the novel, the new, and more concerned with reinforcing the cultural and historical memory and values of the audience. The "novelty" of the oral presentation, then, had to do with how and why familiar stories (and knowledge) were rendered during a particular moment of cultural or political need. In Latini's historical moment, the need was for an allegorical rendering of the invisible, the religious, in relationship to the political realities and impulses of the time. Thus, Latini's (and Dante's) generic predisposition to the familiar forms of religious instruction, which were for the most part based on the oral teaching of Jesus, serves as the basis for the invention of a new kind of allegory, one that was at the same time religious and political—one that was, in other words, double (or twice-told) and, therefore, ironic and deconstructive in relationship to previous allegories.

How does Latini construct his dream vision, his religious/political allegory that was decidedly immediate and rhetorical in its aim? In the introduction to her translation of *Il Tesoretto,* Holloway explains that the poem is a "dream vision, much like Cicero's *Dream of Scipio,*" in which "a visionary experience acts as a frame for the imparting of encyclopedic information." She adds, "The poet as dreamer undergoes an education that is either a success or a failure, an education the reader of the work shares with the protagonist" (xx). But Latini's *Tesoretto* includes more than a continuous dream vision, and the dream vision itself is interrupted by familiar religious genres, such as a sermon and a confession. The poem opens with "an elaborate dedication to a noble reader, a patron so exalted that the ordinary reader assumes that it must be someone great, such as Alfonso the Wise or Saint Louis or Charles of Anjou" (xxi). And the Book itself is troped as a valuable treasure, significant considering that the Guelfs had been unable to pay reparations to the Ghibellines following Montaperti (and during the time of Latini's exile). "It is as if," Holloway writes, "Latini were also saying that books such as the *Tresor* and *Tesoretto*, which fashion a citizen's behavior for the ethical good of the commune, are preferable to treasure chests filled with florins to be paid over to the city's enemies" (xv). The dedication, of course, raises several decidedly ideological questions: Why would Latini, an exiled Guelf republican, want to provide such a literary treasure to a powerful patron, presumably one with little need for advice concerning communal, democratic practice? And would Latini's treasure, in the hands of someone kingly and powerful, be a treasure at all? Ironically, as Holloway points out, the illumination for the dedication page "shows Latini in his master's robes at his writing desk, giving the poem to a humble student figure, not a rich patron" (xxi).

Following the dedication of *Il Tesoretto*, Latini reports his discovery in the Pass of Roncevalles (a place often associated with pilgrimages) of the Guelf defeat at Montaperti and of his own exile. Thus, in the political context of his personal situation and the questionable future of the Florentine Republic, Latini announces his "anguish" over losing himself and losing "the great highway." It is in a "strange wood" that Latini finds himself (as does Dante, later) at the beginning of his dream vision. In this vision, he meets Natura, who instructs him about "God's creation and man's fall" and provides an encyclopedic "survey of the medieval world view"—including "the four humors, the parts of the soul, astronomy, and geography"—and who also "shows Latini the four rivers of Paradise, the Ocean, the Mediterranean Sea, and the Pillars of Hercules" (xxii–xxiii).

Upon leaving Natura, Latini comes to the realm of Philosophy, where he finds not only the Aristotelian virtues, but also "emperors, kings, lords, and professors." In this realm, he overhears the instruction of a young knight, who is being taught by "Gracious Courtesy" how to be not only a good citizen of a "well-ordered city," but also a prudent and effective rhetorician. In Holloway's translation of *Il Tesoretto* (81), Courtesy advises:

> Be sure that Generosity
> Is chief and the greatest
> Of all my craft,
> So that I am worth scarcely anything;
> And if she does not aid me,
> Little would I be pleasing;
> She is my foundation,
> And I her gilding
> And her color and enamel;
> And for him who speaks the truth,
> If we have two separate names,
> We are almost a single thing.
> But to you, beautiful friend,
> First of all I say
> That in your speech
> You should have much precaution:
> Do not speak too much,
> And think beforehand
> Of what you would say,
> For the word that is said
> Never comes back again,
> Just like the arrow
> That goes and does not return.

In this speech by Courtesy, a speech that evokes a deeper value, Generosity, Latini is ironically chipping away at the aristocratic value system held by his putative audience. Commenting on this irony, Holloway notices that the values taught to the young knight "are largely bourgeois virtues, not aristocratic ones." And she suggests that here Latini is working to subvert the received "courtesy book" and to replace it with another sort of book: one "to be read not by members of the nobility, but by members of a bourgeois, republican democracy" (xxiv).

Following the knight's coded, double instruction, Latini begins what Holloway calls the "palinode," entitled in some versions "*La Penetenza* (Penance)." The palinode is a radical break from the dream vision and from its surface offering of a literary treasure. As the palinode begins, Latini redefines his audience as "his Ciceronian friend." It is not clear if Latini's Ciceronian friend is the original patron, but if so, the ensuing sermon and confession are doubly ironic: the sermon advises his friend against relying on worldly treasure (and, presumably, worldly power), and it lists a number of powerful and wealthy figures, among them "Great Julius Caesar" and "Valiant Alexander," who, not considering their own mortality and focused on earthly treasures, wore "the crown / Like base persons," not knowing "the hour or when / Comes that which bears you away, / And which no longer brings / An office or dignity" (125). The sermon enumerates a number of human sins, and it urges his friend to repent of them all. Holloway argues that in the palinode "the poem is both deconstructing and deepening, sloughing off its surface fabling concerning fame to reveal its inner sermon of truth" (xxv). Indeed, after advising his friend, Latini further breaks from his dream vision by recounting his visit to the Friars of Montpellier, thus recovering "the way" from which he had "strayed." In order to overcome what he describes as "a very great fear / And weariness and sorrow / Of body and heart," he thinks of "returning devoutly / To God and the saints, / And very humbly / Confessing my sins / To the priests and the friars" (119). He adds:

> And this, my little book,
> With every other writing
> That I have invented,
> If they contain any vice,
> I commit at all times
> To the friars' correction,
> In order to make the work accord
> With the Christian faith. (119)

Latini's confession focuses on the sin of Pride, and it is with this sin that he associates the very Book he is writing, the *Tesoretto*. In this textually self-referential association of Pride and his Book, Latini calls into question the ontological status of his own work: Is it a treasure, after all, if it pridefully dispenses knowledge to a powerful ruler? Might it be a treasure if it turns, in the palinode, from its ostensible subject and aim? Might it be a treasure if it could serve to advance the Guelf cause and the ideal of a democratic state? Might it be a treasure if it served to do God's will?

After his confession, Latini resumes the dream vision. Returning to "the forest," he rides "so far / That I refound myself / In time one morning / Upon Mount Olympus" (145). In this utterly transformed landscape, having "refound" himself, Latini completes his pilgrimage, seeing below him the land and sea, and around him the air, and beyond him fire. Upon Olympus, he meets Ptolemy, the great astronomer, his beard white and his garments also white. Latini asks for Ptolemy's instruction, Ptolemy smiles, and then, before Ptolemy can answer—the poem abruptly ends. Holloway, her own work intertextual with Kermode's, observes, "We are left without a sense of an ending; the poem has 'deconstructed' itself, and we are jokingly betrayed by our poet storyteller" (Introduction, xxv). But the poem is more than a joke, providing "wisdom" that "lies less with the pagan learning of astronomy and the foreknowledge of a Ptolemy than with Christian preaching and penitence" (xxvi). Commenting on the double, twice-told nature of the poem, and on its intertextual meaning, Holloway suggests: "Latini's *Tesoretto* is a witty joke at the same time that it is a serious sermon. Latini has written, as it were, the 'Art and Remedy of Fame,' thus knitting together Cicero, Ovid, and Boethius" (xxvi). And he also, it might be added, advances Guelf republican values in a coded way at a time when those values had been forced into a context of defeat and exile.

In his second great book, *Li Livres dou Tresor,* also written during his exile, Latini continues to construct a kind of instructional encyclopedia—this time not in the form of an allegorical dream vision in vernacular Italian, but in French and in prose. It is as though the earlier *Il Tesoretto,* with its abrupt, seemingly unfinished ending, serves as a kind of vernacular Italian introduction to a larger work, which concludes with a rhetoric and which, because it was written in the *lingua franca* of the day, was capable of reaching a larger audience. Indeed, *Li Livres dou Tresor* seems to pick up where *Il Tesoretto* leaves off, greatly elaborating, for instance, on the four elements Latini had observed with Ptolemy on top of Olympus. In "A Teacher of Dante," Dole comments on the relationship between Latini's two books: "If the 'Tresors' was written in Paris, 'Il Tesoretto' must have been composed shortly before or at least while he had the 'Gran Tesoro' already planned" (16). Dole then translates Latini at the end of the fourteenth capitolo of his *Tesoretto:* "In this little book I will speak openly [. . .] of Courtesy and Generosity and Loyalty and Valour, of all these I will speak; but of the others I will not promise to speak or to relate; but whoever may wish to find them may search in the "Gran Tesoro" which I will write for those who have their hearts set higher, and there I will make a great endeavour to treat them more at length in the French tongue" (16).

In this, the first chapter of my own Book, my personal search for Latini, I suggested that I would examine his life in relationship to his writing. However, the "Gran Tesoro," which I regard as Latini's greatest contribution to rhetorical history and theory, is simply too important and too vast to be discussed at the conclusion of a chapter. Indeed, it deserves a chapter of its own, and so, like Latini, of this other Book I will not yet speak; but whosoever may wish to find it treated fully may search in my third chapter, which I will write for those who have their hearts set higher, on Latini's theorizing of rhetoric.

But I do not wish to break off this chapter of my search too abruptly, without emphasizing that, like Latini, I have already traveled far, thanks to the guidance of Julia Bolton Holloway's Books. For now, I will leave behind Brunetto Latini the writer, user of brown and purple inks, writer of notarial documents and Books, and I will go searching for Brunetto Latini the teacher of Dante—this before I return to a consideration of *Li Livres dou Tresor,* in which Latini might be found as both writer and teacher of rhetoric.

It does seem appropriate, however, that before leaving Latini's life as an official of Florence and as a writer, I provide a brief memorial to that life, not a description of the column in Santa Maggiore, but the words of the great Florentine chronicler, Giovanni Villani (as translated by Dole):

> In the said year 1294 there died in Florence a worthy citizen named Ser Brunetto Latini, who was a great philosopher and was a supreme master (*sommo maestro*) in rhetoric, both in theory and practice (*tanto in bene sapere dire come in bene dittare*), and it was he who expounded on the rhetoric of Cicero and wrote the good and useful book called "Tesoro" and "Il Tesoretto," and many other works on philosophy and dealing with vices and virtues, and was secretary or speaker of our commune (*dittatore del nostro comune*). (10)

2 Latini, Teacher of Dante, By His Student Damned

In Canto XV of *The Inferno,* Dante, guided by Virgil, enters the Second Zone of the Third Ring of the Seventh Circle of Hell. Here, among the sodomites, he encounters the "spirit" of Bruetto Latini, once his mentor, who, having recognized his former student, cries out, "This is marvelous!" Dante continues:

> That spirit having stretched his arm toward me, 25
> I fixed my eyes upon his baked, brown features,
> so that scorching of his face could not
> prevent my mind from recognizing him; 28
> and lowering my face to meet his face,
> I answered him: "Are you here, Ser Brunetto?"
> And he: "My son, do not mind if Brunetto 31
> Latino lingers for a while with you
> and lets the file he's with pass on ahead."
> I said: "With all my strength, I pray you, stay; 34
> and if you'd have me rest awhile with you,
> I shall, if that please him with whom I go."
> "O son," he said, "whoever of this flock 37
> stops but a moment, stays a hundred years
> and cannot shield himself when fire strikes.
> Therefore move on; below—but close—I'll follow; 40
> and then I shall rejoin my company,
> who go lamenting their eternal sorrows."

Michael Kleine

I did not dare to leave my path for his 43
own level; but I walked with head bent low
as does a man who goes in reverence.
And he began: "What destiny or chance 46
has led you here below before your last
day came, and who is he who shows the way?"
"There, in the sunlit life above," I answered, 49
"before my years were full, I went astray
within a valley. Only yesterday
at dawn I turned my back upon it—but 52
when I was newly lost, he here appeared,
to guide me home again along this path."
And he to me: "If you pursue your star, 55
you cannot fail to reach a splendid harbor,
if in fair life, I judged you properly;
and if I had not died too soon for this, 58
on seeing Heaven was so kind to you,
I should have helped sustain you in your work.
But that malicious, that ungrateful people 61
come down, in ancient times, from Fiesole—
still keeping something of the rock and mountain—
for your good deeds, will be your enemy: 64
and there is cause—among the sour sorbs,
the sweet fig is not meant to bear its fruit,
The world has long since called them blind, a people 67
presumptuous, avaricious, envious;
be sure to cleanse yourself of their foul ways.
Your fortune holds in store such honor for you, 70
one party and the other will be hungry
for you—but keep the grass far from the goat.
For let the beasts of Fiesole find forage 73
among themselves, and leave the plant alone—
if still, among the dung, it rises up—
in which there lives again the sacred seed 76
of those few Romans who remained in Florence

when such a nest of wickedness was built."
"If my desire were answered totally,"
I said to Ser Brunetto, "you'd still be
among, not banished from, humanity.
Within my memory is fixed—and now
moves me—your dear, your kind paternal image
when, in the world above, from time to time
you taught me how man makes himself eternal;
and while I live, my gratitude for that
must always be apparent in my words.
What you have told me of my course, I write:
I keep it with another text, for comment
by one who'll understand, if I may teach her.
One thing alone I'd have you plainly see:
so long as I am not rebuked by conscience,
I stand prepared by Fortune, come what may.
My ears find no new pledge in that prediction;
therefore, let Fortune turn her wheel as she
may please, and let the peasant turn his mattock."
At this, my master turned his head around
and toward the right, and looked at me and said:
"He who takes note of this has listened well."
But nonetheless, my talk with Ser Brunetto
continues, and I ask of him who are
his comrades of repute and excellence.
And he to me: "To know of some is good;
but for the rest, silence is to be praised;
the time we have is short for so much talk.
In brief, know that my company has clerics
and men of letters and of fame—and all
were stained by one same sin upon the earth.
That sorry crowd holds Priscian and Francesco
d'Accorso; and among them you can see,
if you have any longing for such scurf,
the one the Servant of his Servants sent

from the Arno to the Bacchiglione's banks,
and there he left his tendons strained by sin.
I would say more; but both my walk and words   115
must not be longer, for—beyond—I see
new smoke emerging from the sandy bed.
Now people come with whom I must not be.   118
Let my *Tesoro*, in which I still live,
be precious to you; and I ask no more."
And then he turned and seemed like one of those   121
who race across the fields to win the green
cloth at Verona; of those runners, he
appeared to be the winner, not the loser.   124

In my search for Latini, I have spent much time reading and rereading the Allen Mandelbaum translation of Canto XV of the *Inferno* that I provide above, nearly in its entirety. It was not until just now, however, as I copied the text into the memory of my word processor, that I felt, so deeply, Dante's terrible ambivalence about his mentor, Latini. Indeed, by participating in the classical and medieval pedagogy of imitation, in which great texts were copied word for word by the student, I somehow became the student of the student of Latini. Was this the kind of instruction that Dante himself received? Would he have copied down parts of the *Epistolarium*, which Latini helped to shape, or Latini's *Tesoro* that he finds in hell? In copying a passage from a translation of Dante's Book, I understood, at last, the illuminations and figurations of the "teacher" in medieval manuscripts. Often we see the teacher not in the center, but off to the side with the students; in the privileged center is the text, the Book, presumably the source of what is known and, in effect, the primary educator of both the teacher and his students. In an illumination associated with *Il Tesoretto*, we see Latini, the teacher, handing over his book to the reader, presumably a student. The implication is now clear to me: in copying the Book, in "twice writing it," the student is brought into a special relationship with it and with its intertextual power. In the future, that student will write not something original, but a palimpsest upon the manuscript that served to teach him.

So it is in this role as student copyist and would-be pilgrim that I will begin my discussion of Latini as teacher of Dante, heeding carefully Dante's words and aware that my transcription is no doubt teaching me to write my own Book, my own pilgrimage tale. However, I will also find in the words of Latini, given to him by Dante, the generous and human teacher for whom I search, one who not only influenced his student during his life, but who also still enjoys his student's affection and high regard following his death. And this in spite of Dante's decision to include his mentor in the Seventh Circle of Hell among the sodomites.

What do I learn about Dante by copying a translation of his poetry? As copyist, I feel, with Dante, his clear identification with his mentor in the valuation of a Roman past—indeed, his crediting of Latini with understanding that any Guelf good enjoyed by the citizens of Florence is enjoyed in spite of "the beasts of Fiesole" (a little hill town above Florence, founded by the Etruscans) and because of "those few Romans who remained in Florence":

> For let the beasts of Fiesole find forage 73
> among themselves, and leave the plant alone—
> if still, among the dung, it rises up—
> in which there lives again the sacred seed 76
> of those few Romans who remained in Florence
> when such a nest of wickedness was built.

At the same time, thanks to Holloway's textual guidance, I understand that the "Rome" valued by Dante was more the Rome of the Empire, whereas the Rome of Latini was most certainly the Rome of the Republic. In his effort to include his teacher in his own political vision, Dante suggests that it is not by his doing, not by his condemnation, that Latini finds himself in hell, with "baked, brown features." Indeed, Dante suggests that it is some force beyond his control that separates Latini from his personal desire to see his mentor as a political and cultural affiliate:

> "If my desire were answered totally," 79
> I said to Ser Brunetto, "you'd still be
> among, not banished from, humanity."

As I copied these lines, I wondered just whose desire it was that banished Latini from Dante's vision of what is essential to both humanity and salvation. Perhaps the explanation of Latini's damnation may have something to do with a pun on Brunetto's "brown-ness," a color that Dante earlier associated (in Canto XIII of *The Inferno*) with chancery ink. If so, the "baked, brown features" may evoke, for Dante, not the rhetorical contributions of his mentor, but the republican motives of his civic and political writing, motives that necessarily lead, from an imperial point of view (influenced by Dante's other mentors, Aristotle and Virgil), to Latini's damnation.

In Canto XV, Dante speaks for himself and for his mentor. Speaking as a former student, Dante expresses profound gratitude for his mentor and remembers, fondly, his "paternal image" and the way Latini taught him "from time to time [. . .] how man makes himself eternal":

> Within my memory is fixed—and now 82
> moves me—your dear, your kind paternal image
> when, in the world above, from time to time
> you taught me how man makes himself eternal; 85
> and while I live, my gratitude for that
> must always be apparent in my words.

With Dante, I feel the anguish of an inspired student, one who credits his mentor with important teaching, but who also sees his teacher's extra-curricular writing and work as decidedly wrong-minded, every bit as "un-natural" as sodomy, perhaps even a regression to the wickedness of the "beasts of Fiesole."

And now I turn to feel the teacherly impulses of Latini, the way he nurtured and brought to fruition the very rhetoric and writing in which he is condemned to hell. Dante has Latini say:

> And he to me: "If you pursue your star, 55
> you cannot fail to reach a splendid harbor,
> if in fair life, I judged you properly;
> and if I had not died too soon for this, 58
> on seeing Heaven was so kind to you,
> I should have helped sustain you in your work."

In Latini's words, given to him by his student, I feel the very real impulses and motives of a teacher, concerned more with the work and success of his student than with his own work and success. Shifting from my student copyist role to my role as a teacher of writing, I feel, in Dante's appreciation, the crediting of what it is that many teachers, particularly teachers of writing, most desire: the brilliance and importance of the words written by their students.

The irony in Canto XV is profound. In it, we find the fruition of Latini's teaching in the written words of his student, Dante. And yet it is, somehow, the result of great teaching that has textually damned the teacher. Furthermore, we find that Latini's teaching text is somehow with him in hell, that the scattered pages of his *Tesoro*—the very work that perhaps best taught Dante—burn with him there. Latini requests:

> Let my *Tesoro*, in which I still live,
> be precious to you; and I ask no more.

How can this be? How can we begin to understand what it was, exactly, that Latini taught to his student "from time to time"—and why it was, if not for the "sin" of sodomy, that the teacher (and his manuscript) needed to be assigned to hell? Was Dante's motive perhaps ideological? In my own life as a teacher of persuasive writing, I have often found, in some of the best writing produced by my students, ideological positions not my own, indeed, the articulation of arguments that would, by virtue of their underlying values, tend to consign what I most deeply believe to a kind of necessary ideological damnation. How to understand all of this—from a rhetorical perspective, yes, but also from a personal pedagogical perspective? The only path that appears to me here is one that forks, one that requires two pilgrim walks: one walk might consider what and how Latini taught his student, Dante—and another walk might consider why the teacher, and the political ideology of the teacher, needed to be condemned to *The Inferno*. By taking both paths, I hope I will be able to move beyond what is, for me, the central obstacle in finding the figure, the figuration, for whom I search. I will argue that it is an obstacle that has everything to do with the teacher's Pride—with the very sin by which Latini condemns his own literal text in *Il Tesoretto*. I will also argue that, for both Latini and Dante, the rhetorical heart of Latini's teaching, of his Books, transcends its own material and historical substance and provides a third path, a "path that does not stray."

The First Path—Latini's Teaching of Dante

As Holloway points out in her Introduction to her translation of *Il Tesoretto*, "We do not know whether Dante was a student of Brunetto Latini—at least in the sense that 'teacher' has for us now." She adds, "It is likely that Latini and Dante's relationship was informal—shall we say like that of Plato to Socrates and of Cicero's circle in Tusculum?—

consisting of hour-long conversations in Florentine piazzas" (xvii). But in striving to understand how it was that Latini taught Dante, we might look beyond the possibility of peripatetic instruction and consider, especially, the sort of textual and intertextual instruction that Latini probably provided for his student; for it is in texts that we can best understand, if not how, at least what it was that Latini taught. And it is in Dante's great text, *The Divine Comedy,* that we can best understand what was learned, what was kept as golden treasure, and what was rejected and damned as dross.

Based upon her examination of manuscripts in Florence, Holloway believes that, in terms of Latini's textual teaching of Dante, the key text would have been not Latini's French *Tresor,* but a version written in vernacular Italian, the *Tesoro,* once erroneously attributed to a Ghibelline rhetorician and ethicist, Bono Giamboni. But as a teaching text, the *Tesoro* was produced in a way that links it to oral instruction, to lecture. Holloway explains in *Twice-Told Tales*: "Both the *Tresor* and the *Tesoro* texts appear to be highly oral, the second even more so than the first, as if they were dictated rather than copied." Thus, "the genre in which Brunetto wrote was really that of the university lecture, to be copied down by students, as indeed had been the case with the teachings of Aristotle in the Greek and Arabic worlds" (10). In such a way, Latini may have both walked and talked with his student, Dante, and also "lectured" to him.

If we accept the notion of intertextuality, then the answer to the question "What did Latini teach to Dante?" might be, quite simply, found in the nature and substance of the texts produced by Dante. But a more specific answer might be found in Marcia Colish's helpful book, *The Mirror of Language: A Study in the Medieval Theory of Language:* the great importance of Latini's teaching can be found not only in the poetic intertextual resonances of *Il Tesoretto* and

The Divine Comedy, but also in Dante's application of his teacher's theoretical insistence on the linkage of poetry with didactic persuasion. In her consideration of Latini's notion of the "competence" of rhetoric, advanced in his French *Tresor,* Colish writes:

> Brunetto states that it (competence) has cognizance of matters both private and public. It is used 'to "induce belief" (*por faire croire*), to praise and to blame, and to hold counsel on any needful matter, or about anything that requires judgment. Anything can be dealt with by rhetoric so long as it is written or spoken; thus rhetoric covers prose, poetry, and the *ars dictaminis.* (164)

She further argues, "Brunetto links rhetoric, including poetry, to wisdom and virtue, and also to a specific kind of political morality which flows from a specific set of political institutions, those of the Italian city-state of his own day" (165). And, indeed, *The Divine Comedy* can be read not only as a dream vision, as poetry, but also, in its praising and blaming of political figures, as a work of didactic, ceremonial persuasion.

But *The Divine Comedy* is also a work that reflects a moral and spiritual vision, and it is, ironically, Latini himself who, by Dante's own admission, "taught" him "how man makes himself eternal." At the heart of this moral vision is an aversion, shared by both teacher and student, to the quest for worldly Fame, which in the medieval world, as Holloway reminds, is tantamount to Pride, "and as such is the root of all sin." Pride, remember, was the sin that prompted Latini to call his writerly motives and his own material product, *Il Tesoretto,* into question. In her Introduction to her translation of that product, Holloway comments on the irony of Dante's acknowledgement of what his teacher taught him: "Dante seems foolishly to say that he has learned from Latini 'come l'uom s'eterna," which she interprets and glosses "how man makes himself eternal—by means of worldly fame." She adds, commenting on Dante's "let Fortune turn her wheel just as she pleases" (lines 95–96) that "Dante's surface text has perverted his Master's teachings, and those of Cicero and Boethius," for "if he is literally saying that, he is indeed a fallen Adam," then "he would only be correct were he to mean he would, in the Stoic and Christian manner, have nothing to do with Fortune and her Wheel, but instead would quest after Blessedness, or Beatrice" (xxvii). Thus, in the deep intertextual ironies of Canto XV, we can hear Dante adverting to the very real moral values of his teacher, but at the same time, like his teacher, falling into the trap by which the physical text, in its manifestation of Pride and its quest for Fame, provides only an earthly treasure and a cause for damnation of both writer and product. By "defaming" his teacher and his teacher's work, Dante indirectly condemns his own perversion of his Master's teachings, and his own quest for worldly Fame, to the same hell through which he travels as a pilgrim and in which he finds his teacher.

If we move beyond the rhetorical values and the textual ironies that Latini taught, we might also come to see Latini as a teacher of encyclopedic knowledge, and also of poetic formal and stylistic proclivities. In their encyclopedia components, *Il Tesoretto* and, especially, *Li Livres dou Tresor* attempt to pass on not only what was then known of the natural order, but also political and social history. In *Twice-Told Tales,* Holloway credits Latini with teaching Dante a "mental theatre of memory acquired most likely from Latino of thirteenth-century archives." That "theatre of memory," which was employed by Dante as he wrote during his own exile, was an "ancient form of a computer retrieval system." Dante used the knowledge and retrieval system he learned from his mentor to create "out of the often sordid criminality of the past, magnificent poetry, the dead but true Latin archival documents palimpsesting" Dante's "fictional, yet intensely alive" poetry (4). As an encyclopedia, as a poetic presentation of what was "known," Dante's *The Divine Comedy* manifests the same sort of hierarchical ordering and listing characteristic of Latini's Books, a nearly hypertextual (and decidedly intertextual) web of historical and "scientific" facts. It is very possible that Dante learned the branching, tree-like structures for both the remembering and representation of "knowledge" (those structures called *"alberi,"* or trees, in Latini's *La Rettorica*) from his mentor, whose organizational impulses and accomplishments preceded his own. Compositionists familiar with the cognitivist agenda that drove writing research and teaching a little over twenty years ago, especially the work of Linda Flower, are probably struck, as I am, by Latini's interest in the hierarchical storage and retrieval of information—and by his problem-solving approach to organizing (in his *"alberi"*) knowledge structures. Flower proposed pedagogical strategies that involved helping students use "trees" to plan written discourse. In my own case, I still use "treeing" as a visual strategy to help students conceptualize what they are reading and writing. Now I see that this strategy probably can be traced back at least to Latini.

Although the narrative shape of the pilgrimage tale predates Latini, indeed is mythological and Biblical, the particular landscape of Dante's dream vision, especially its starting point, can be attributed to his teacher. In "A Teacher of Dante," Dole comments: "We know nothing of Brunetto as an instructor, but the debt that Dante owed to him as a poet is easily demonstrated" (5). To demonstrate that debt, Dole focuses not on *Li Livres dou Tresor,* but on *Il Tesoretto,* of which he writes: "A very superficial examination will show that Dante did not hesitate to imitate Brunetto Latini in many curious little details" (14). He adds: "It is evident, then, that Brunetto felt a greater tenderness for his poetical thesaurus than for his French one; that Dante took from the dedication the recommendation to his patron to treat it as a treasure" (17). In particular, Dole notices that *The Inferno* begins in exactly the same way that *Il Tesoretto*, following its dedication, begins—in the landscape of a "strange wood," for Latini, and in the landscape of a "dark wood," for Dante. Holloway, too, notices Dante's indebtedness to Latini. Both Latini and Dante, in their poetic dream visions, have lost their respective ways, and both find themselves "lost." She writes in her Introduction to her translation of *Il Tesoretto:* "Dante here is borrowing consciously from Latini, and is carrying out a tribute to his Master—though he does place him in Hell. Moreover, Dante's borrowing of Latini's opening gives to his own pilgrim poem's beginning the shadowy configuration of that valley of the shadow of death, the Pass of Roncesvalles, famous both for Roland's ill-fated battle with the Saracens and also for its pilgrimage road to the shrine of Santiago de Compostela" (xxii).

Finally, I look to Latini's teaching of eloquence and style. Marcia Colish, like Holloway, strongly associates Latini's teaching with the teaching of his own rhetorical mentor, Cicero. She writes: "Brunetto follows Cicero in insisting [. . .] eloquence is necessary for the proper conduct of political life" (163). She credits to Cicero, and to his student, Latini, the notion that "wisdom joined to eloquence engenders goodness" (163–64). For Latini, first, and then for his student, Dante, eloquence might be discovered in vernacular Italian, not merely in Latin. Commenting on Latini's effort to revive Ciceronian eloquence and style, Holloway writes: "It was necessary for him to conquer it into the lowly vernacular, to make it available to the people, such as bankers and merchants who so intensely participated in Florentine government—even when in exile" (*Twice-Told Tales,* 262). However, Colish argues that Dante abandons "the idea of poetry as decoration" (165). Indeed, in stylistic matters, Dante looks to another mentor, "Virgil, whom Dante acknowledges in the *Comedy* as the light and honor of the other poets, his master and author, and the source of his own style, and whom he takes as his guide through Hell and Purgatory" (162). Holloway sees in Canto XV, beyond the damnation of Latini, a "curious debasement and putdown" of Latini's style, which "seems to be Dante's debasement, too, of the republicans Cicero and Latino, in preference to the grandiloquent style of imperial Virgil" (297).

And so, in considering how and what Latini taught Dante, it is possible to find the profound influence of teacher upon student. But it is also possible to find Dante's rejection of his teacher's teacher, his preference of imperial Aristotle and Virgil to republican Cicero. In short, though Latini taught his student how to write persuasively and brilliantly, he failed to impart his deeply held ideological values.

The Second Path—Dante's Damnation of His Teacher

As a teacher of rhetoric and writing, I am troubled, of course, by Dante's defaming and damnation of his own teacher of rhetorical practice. Even more troubling is that there is no compelling historical evidence that the "runners" with whom Latini is grouped (figures associated with philosophy), the other group of runners (figures associated with political action), and Latini himself are guilty of the medieval sin of sodomy. In a recent essay, "The Pose of the Queer: Dante's Gaze, Brunetto Latini's Body," Michael Camille argues against revisionist readings of Canto XV, which suggest that Dante's portrayal of Latini as a sodomite in fact serves as a metaphor for some other offense. Camille suggests that these revisionist readings evince a fear of the sodomitic body. His argument, however, is based on a fourteenth-century manuscript illustration of Latini and Dante, itself a reading and representation of Canto XV. Nevertheless, the question remains: if not for the medieval "sin" of sodomy, why would a clearly successful writer consign his mentor to hell, and this despite Dante's clear affection and high regard for Latini?

I turn again to Holloway for guidance in this matter. In her introduction to her translation of *Il Tesoretto*, she provides a brief history of scholarly efforts to account for Latini's damnation:

> Early commentators justified Dante's charge of sodomy by noting that this was a common problem between teachers and students. Andre Pezard argues that Dante condemns Latini not for homosexuality, but for blasphemy, in particular for blaspheming against the Italian language by writing in French. Richard Kay makes the more likely claim that Dante condemns Latini for his Guelph idolatry of Florence as a Republic, rather than being a Ghibelline advocate of Empire. Thomas Werge states that Dante condemns Latini because Latini's *Tesoro* is a worldly quest for fame, for treasure laid up on Earth rather than in Heaven. Jeffrey Richards notes that Latini and his *Tesoro* are burned in the flames of Hell by Dante, who is jokingly carrying out his Master's instructions given in *Tesoretto* 103–12. (xiv)

With Holloway, I believe that Richard Kay's argument is the most convincing, suggesting as it does that what Dante found most "unnatural" about his mentor was his ideological stance in *Li Livres dou Tresor*. And so, for a while, Kay will guide my journey down my "second path."

In a brilliant essay entitled "The Sin of Brunetto Latini," Kay reasons deductively, using Dante's philosophy having to do with Nature and government as warrant, that Latini's "sin" was, indeed, a sin against Nature, but not a sin of the flesh; instead it was a sin against the "natural" political order and, thus, a sin against God. Kay begins his argument by noticing that Virgil maps, in Canto XI, the Three Rings of the Seventh Circle of Hell before he and Dante arrive at the Third Ring in Canto XV, where Latini is discovered:

> One can be violent against the Godhead,   46
> one's heart denying and blaspheming Him
> and scorning nature and the good in her;
> so, with this sign, the smallest ring has sealed   49
> both Sodom and Cahors and all of those
> who speak in passionate contempt of God.

Although the map clearly indicates that the Seventh Circle is the general area in which sins of violence are punished, and that the Third Ring is the particular area in which those sins represent violence "against the Godhead," Kay argues that Virgil's characterization of the Third Ring is ambiguous. While it seems to be the case that blasphemers, usurers, and sodomites are being punished there, it appears that in addition there may be others present in the Third Ring ("and all of those / who speak in passionate contempt of God"). Thus, though Latini is categorized among those who have violently sinned against God, it is not at all clear that he is being punished for the sin of sodomy.

Kay suggests that, beyond the map provided by Virgil, the best way to understand Latini's sin is to consider his associates and the philosophical principle that might be driving Dante's sense of whom he must damn along the path of his pilgrimage. (Implicit, I think, is the possibility that

Dante believed that, had he retained his own association with Latini, he might have been incapable of moving, both spiritually and textually, beyond *The Inferno* and toward *The Paradiso*.)

Kay sees the "runners," damned to run in the Second Zone of the Third Ring for eternity, as belonging to two mutually exclusive groups (the two groups will have nothing to do with each other), related only at a higher level of the organization of hell. In the first group, to which Latini belongs, are "clerics / and men of letters and of fame" (Canto XV, lines 106–107). Only three other members of Latini's group are mentioned: Priscian, a Latin grammarian; Francessco d'Accorso, a professor of Roman law; and a bishop, whom Latini does not think worthy of naming. As Kay notes, all four members of this group conform to Brunetto's definition: the first three were laymen famous for their learning; the bishop was a clergyman infamous for his lack of it" (5). The other group of runners (Dante mentions three of them by name in Canto XVI) were Florentine politicians, all having in common "their prominence in Florentine politics, and particularly in the Guelf party" (6). Taxonomically, then, Dante divides the running sinners on the basis of their vocations, but on a higher level, the level of the Ring, they are, along with the blasphemers, all sinners against God. And at a higher level yet, the level of the Circle, they are, along with murderers and suicides, guilty of violent sins, both against Nature and God.

The hierarchically organized architecture of hell is difficult to understand without "*alberi,*" without trees. Below, in the spirit of Latini's attraction toward hierarchical representations of knowledge and of Dante's taxonomic approach to sin, I provide a tree of my own to make sense out the taxonomy in which Latini's sin is included.

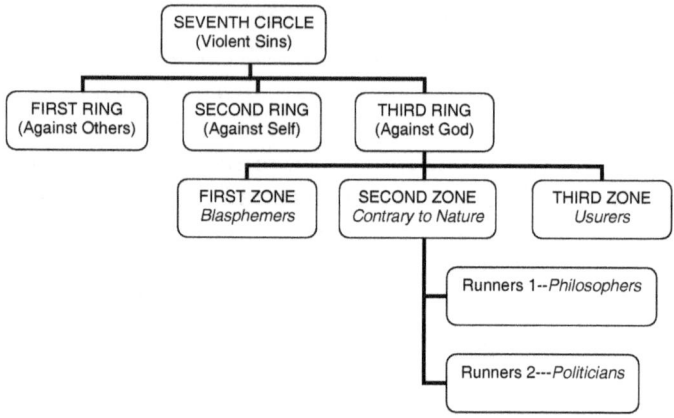

Albero 1: Dante's organization of the Seventh Circle of Hell.

As Kay suggests, the runners, as opposed to the other sinners in the Seventh Circle, are grouped not by sin, but by vocation. Moreover, all of the runners, aside from the bishop, had been held in high regard by their Florentine (and Guelf) contemporaries. Kay wonders: "In what sense could such honorable men be said to have sinned against nature?" (7). He suggests that to answer this, we need to "know how scholarship and statesmanship are related to Dante's conception of nature" (8), which Kay indicates is outlined in the concluding chapter of Dante's *On Monarchy*.

Dante's conception of human nature again can be represented hierarchically, as shown in *Albero* 2. Every person has two parts—body and soul, each of which has separate virtues and each of which is guided by separate goals (and by separate higher authorities). In matters of the body, of "Nature," the virtue of intellect is guided by the reasoning of philosophers, while the virtue of the will needs to be controlled by the power of an emperor. However, in matters of the soul, the three great theological virtues (faith, hope, and charity) are guided by representatives of God, such as Christ and his disciples. These virtues are attained on earth only through grace, and they have to do more with the guidance of the pope than with the control of the emperor.

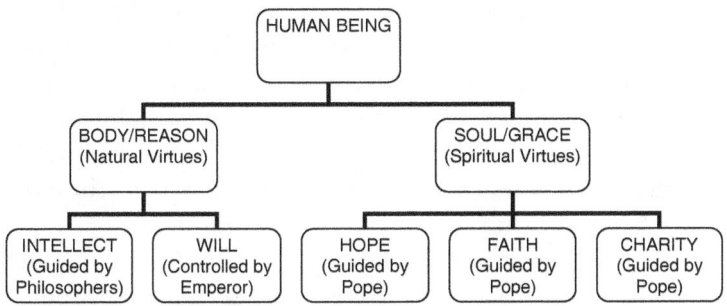

Albero 2: Medieval conception of the guidance and control of the Human Being.

Kay argues that it is in relationship to Dante's hierarchical conceptualization of man that Latini's "sin against nature" can be understood, for it is only the runners (the philosophers and the politicians) who "are violent against nature alone" (11). He explains that "they do violence to God, to use Virgil's words, by 'disdaining nature and its goodness' (*Inf.* XI, 48). In place of the natural authority, which they do not acknowledge, they will set up for themselves an *un*natural authority." Thus, "any unnatural authority" is by necessity perverse, "a denial either of the true authority of philosophy over the intellect or of the true authority of the empire over the will" (11). As an intellectual, a philosopher, and a writer, Latini has committed an intellectual sin by philosophically (and intellectually) advocating republican and Ciceronian values, and by encouraging the kind of anti-imperial political praxis represented by the second group of runners. Like the politicians, Latini is motivated more by Pride (and a quest for Fame) than he is by obedience to the natural virtues ordained by God. Indeed, as Kay points out, Dante shows Latini (in Canto XV) urging Dante "to apply his intellectual gifts, to live the life of letters as Brunetto himself has done"; moreover, he shows Latini reassuring him that "fortune has reserved for Dante such honor that he will become the envy of his fellow Florentines" and that "he has been so richly endowed by nature that he can expect to achieve great things, for which fame shall be his reward" (16). In other words, in his praise of Dante, Latini emphasizes the fame of his student rather than his goodness, and in so doing he reveals that "the ideals he imputes to Dante are in fact his own" (17).

Driving Latini's intellectual (and pedagogical) sin against nature is an underlying, more egregious sin, Pride, which Latini himself confessed in *Il Tesoretto*. Indeed, it is the sin of Pride that nudges Latini to recommend to Dante, in his teacherly absence, to look to the *Tesoro* as a guide. In this recommendation, Latini seems to be asserting his centrality as Dante's teacher—not only as the one who taught him temporally, "from time to time," but also as the one who might teach Dante (and others) eternally, the *Tesoro* itself becoming an immortal textual teacher. Reflecting on Dante's characterization of his mentor, Kay writes:

> As is often the case with advisers who seek to live through their advisees, Brunetto tends to maximize his own influence on Dante and to exclude that of all others. Brunetto would himself have been the best guide in Dante's work, he seems to say, but since he is no longer available, Dante should follow his star to the goal that Brunetto had foreseen, and in default of the master himself, the *Tresor* will guide him. There is the implicit suggestion that Virgil's intervention was not altogether necessary, as indeed it was not, in order for Dante to achieve the goal that Brunetto

had in mind. The more Dante's greatness is the product of Brunetto's, the better the maestro will like it. (17)

However, Dante will abandon his mentor in Canto XV, and he will move on toward Paradise, accompanied not by republican Latini, but by imperial Virgil. Latini's "perversion" of natural philosophy has much to do, of course, with the teaching of his own mentor, Cicero. For Dante, then, his defamation of his actual teacher, Latini, who twice calls Dante "his son," might be seen in terms of a search for another father, a kind of spiritual teacher, figured by Virgil. In turning from Latini, Dante also turns from Cicero, presumably to embrace the more conservative rhetorical and political views of philosophers advocating empire, such as Aristotle.

As Dante leaves his mentor behind in the *Inferno,* he also leaves, at least for now, Latini's *Tesoro,* presumably based on Latini's great treatise *Li Livres dou Tresor.* Perhaps for Dante, Latini's Book was both the source and the emblem of rhetoric put to bad use. In his discussion of *Li Livres dou Treso*r, Kay points out that Book 3 is divided into two parts, one treating rhetoric and one treating political science. Insofar as Dante himself strove to be a virtuous public servant, he must have appreciated Latini's linkage of rhetoric to governance. However, as Kay puts it, "In a manual for the instruction of a medieval monarch, this stress on rhetoric for the ruler might seem to be a strange anachronism, but when we turn to the culminating treatise on political science proper, we discover that rhetoric is in fact essential to the ruler for whom Brunetto wrote." And, as Dante must have understood, "the head of state that he (Latini) had in mind was not a feudal monarch, but the elected ruler of a thirteenth-century Italian city-state, the official known as the podesta" (19). Latini's sin against nature, then, driven by Pride and arrogance, was a sin against the intent of God, inscribed in his Book and taught to his students. For Dante, the *Tresor* was in many ways the kind of earthly treasure that was criticized in the gospel of Matthew.

It was not, therefore, a sin of the flesh that constrained Dante to assign his mentor and friend to the Seventh Circle of Hell; instead it was a sin of Pride and ideological perversion of natural philosophy, a sin manifested most in Latini's teaching and writing. Kay sums up Dante's damnation of Latini: "For what was Brunetto Latini if not a rhetorician dedicated to the cause of the Florentine Guelfs? He is in Hell because the poet profoundly believed that such a life constituted a tragic waste of natural talent, which is misdirected against the imperial order sanctioned by God and established by Him in nature itself" (22). Insofar as Latini palimpsested his own mentor's writing, we can assume that Cicero, Latini's column and unstagnant fountain, might also be found in the Seventh Circle of Hell, his column shattered, his fountain dry.

The Third Path—Material/Historical Transcendence of the "Treasure"

At the risk of seeming hopelessly Platonic, I seek now a third path, one that might lead me from a historically situated and shadowy view of Latini as teacher of Dante and as author of material manuscripts hidden away in archives. On this pilgrim path, which leads to reflection on my own life as a teacher of writing, and also on the writing of my own Book, I search for a Latini who deserves to transcend historical damnation and obscurity, and I search for a *Tresor* that might live on, not only for Dante, but for my colleagues who teach rhetoric and writing in the twenty-first century, and also for my students. It is a path that will lead, finally, to a focused consideration of Latini's *Tresor* in the next chapter and that will hand that important work over not to a *podesta*, but to those who teach deliberative rhetoric today,

Latini, Teacher of Dante

believing that it might enable their students to participate ethically and effectively in the kind of public discourse that is essential to the health and progress of a democracy.

Guided by Holloway and Kay, and also by Latini and Dante, just what have I learned about myself as a teacher of writing? Certainly I have learned that it is the writing teacher's fate to prepare students to write texts that may or may not participate in the ideology of the teacher. If I teach writing well, then I must be prepared to read, in my students' writing, not the texts that I might write, but the texts that they must write in order to be fully enfranchised, to participate thoughtfully and authentically in the civic and political debates that are at the heart of a democracy. Too, I have learned that I must not be prideful and arrogant, crediting myself, and myself alone, for the written successes of my students. Although I might hope for their success—indeed, even hope that they surpass my instruction and the quality of my own writing—I must avoid the kind of prideful paternalism that we see in Latini as he is portrayed by Dante. I have learned to embrace the obscurity of the writing teacher, for it is the obscure teacher, residing in the margins of his or her own classroom and centering the texts of others, who might best create a space in which intertextuality and debate, not the professions of the teacher, become the heart of what is deeply learned and practiced.

Dante ends his *Paradiso* with these lines:

> Here force failed my high fantasy; but my   142
> desire and will were moved already—like
> a wheel revolving uniformly—by
> the Love that moves the sun and the other stars.   145

I am not sure what "Love" might mean when it informs the practice of the writing teacher. But as a teacher deeply influenced by the work of Paulo Freire, especially *Pedagogy of the Oppressed,* I go to his notion of teacherly love. Such love, Freire shows us, has to do with a refusal to "objectify" our students. Instead of lecturing to them (and dispensing our privileged knowledge as a kind of capital that we own and loan out), it would have us turn to the problems that concern them, sharing with them a literacy that might "liberate" them from the kind of "banking" pedagogy that inevitably oppresses not only the students, but also their teachers. Such a loving pedagogy would be founded not on pride in what we know, and pride in our own teaching, but on humility and inter-subjective relationships with our students.

Although Dante portrays his teacher as a prideful representative of the "banking" tradition, we can also find in Latini's work as both a teacher of writing and as a rhetorical theorist a clear impulse toward the kind of pedagogy recommended by Freire. Latini's effort to vernacularize and demystify not only chancery documents, but also rhetorical theory, evince a decidedly liberatory impulse. In my personal search for Latini, I find, for the time being, an incredibly complex human being—prideful, at times, but also deeply committed to republican values of political inclusion and democratic praxis. He models for me, as does his mentor, Cicero, the liberating potential of a rhetoric aimed at encouraging rather than silencing public debate and participation. The image of Latini that I now hold both cautions and encourages me: he cautions me to be wary of paternalistic impulses; he encourages me to "vernacularize" my teaching and to palimpsest my version of deliberative rhetoric on liberatory rhetorics of the past, including both *De Inventione* and *Li Livres dou Tresor*.

As for writing my own Book, *Searching for Latini,* the subject of my search, though long dead, teaches me to write with humility. Such humility involves seeking appropriate guides, such as Holloway, who might lead me in this, my pilgrimage. I am not a medievalist. I am not an Italian historian. I speak Italian poorly. Thus, if I am to write my Book in good faith, I must acknowledge that it is, if anything, a palimpsest, writing that I am endeavoring to do on top of the truly authoritative texts of others. In my own case, I write over the writing of Holloway, who in turn has written over the writing of Latini, who in turn has written over the writing of Cicero. Not twice-written, but at least quadruple-written, my writing is, indeed, the writing of a student, the writing of a pilgrim.

In the next chapter, I will suggest that Latini's *Tresor* is much more than an earthly treasure—an exilic and marginal document, relevant only to the exigence and *kairos* from which, and in which, it was written over eight-hundred years ago. Indeed, if we listen carefully, we can find words that might speak to us in our post-9/11 world. Dante himself, after he had traveled from *Inferno* to *Paradiso*, now writing from a condition of great humility and grace, suggests that the texts he had once seen as earthly and scattered—perhaps the pages of the *Tresor,* even—might become fully meaningful and transcendent, fully unified and bound by the kind of love that transcends ideology, that is capable of hearing the diverse human voices that speak to us:

> O grace abounding, through which I presumed   82
> to set my eyes on the Eternal Light
> so long that I spent all my sight on it!
>   In its profundity I saw—ingathered   85
> and bound by love into one single volume—
> what, in the universe, seems separate, scattered:
> substances, accidents, and dispositions   88
> as if conjoined—in such a way that what
> I tell is only rudimentary. (*Paradiso*)

Acknowledging that "what I tell is only rudimentary," I want to say that Latini's *Tresor* seems worthy of being "ingathered,'" included in the here and now of our teaching of rhetoric and writing. In so saying, I mean to suggest that Latini produced something far more enduring than an earthly treasure, and that he has much to teach to us today.

3 The Currency of Latini's Rhetorical Treasure

I have so far lamented the obscurity of Brunetto Latini, and I have suggested his worthiness as both a teacher of persuasion and a rhetorical theorist. In my personal search for Latini, I have found him not only in translations of his own surviving texts, but also in the *Divine Comedy* and in a rather extensive historical and critical literature. I have learned that he is less obscure among medievalists and European scholars and more obscure among contemporary American rhetoricians and teachers of writing. My purpose in searching for Latini, then, has evolved since I began my personal pilgrimage: it seems, now, to have to do with searching for Latini, yes, but also with importing his work (and the work of significant Latini scholars) into my own research and teaching community, with "ingathering" his "treasure," his scattered pages, into the contemporary American canon of western rhetorical history and theory. Julia Bolton Holloway, who has been the principal guide in my search, suggests that Latini's obscurity among American rhetoricians has much to do with the inaccessibility of his work, and she has endeavored to remedy this by joining with others working to translate Latini into English. And yet, American rhetoricians do have what I want to call "vernacular access" to what well may be Latini's greatest contribution to rhetorical theory, *Li Livres dou Tresor,* written in French, the *lingua franca* of his day, during his exile from

Florence. Thanks to the work of Chabaille (1863) and, especially, Carmody (1947), we have a more or less stable and authoritative version of Latini's "treasure," his "*Tresor*." And thanks to an English translation of Carmody's text, done by Paul Barrette and Spurgeon Baldwin, and published in 1993, American rhetoricians can gain a sense of the substance and significance of Latini's translating (and palimpsesting) of Cicero's *De Inventione*.

In the following pages of this third chapter of my own Book, I will become a sort of apologist, not only apologizing literally for American neglect of one of the most significant figures in western rhetorical history, but also advocating for a turn away from our neglect and a turn toward reading and recognizing a historical figure who has the potential to teach us much in our own post-9/11 world. Indeed, it is Latini who might best remind us, as rhetoricians and teachers, of the literacy-based rhetoric that promotes and guides the kind of ethical, deliberative, and liberatory discourse that is essential to democratic and inclusive self governance.

In their introduction to their translation of *Li Livres dou Tresor*, Barrette and Baldwin notice contemporary neglect of Latini, suggesting that he "will be familiar to most modern readers only because he was Dante's teacher" (vii), but they also emphasize that Latini's *Tresor* was extremely popular and widely read as the Renaissance began to unfold, and this despite the demise of its genre, "a compendium of primarily classical material, following in a long tradition of such collections, with origins in late Antiquity and the early Middle Ages, a genre which was to finally die in the Renaissance" (viii). Indeed, it is possible, as James East argues in "Brunetto Latini's Rhetoric of Letter Writing" (one of the few American appreciations of Latini, published in 1968 in *The Quarterly Journal of Speech*), that the *Tresor* was "one of the two most popular books of knowledge of the Middle Ages" and that it "was second in popularity only to a Latin

The Currency of Latini's Rhetorical Treasure

encyclopedia called *Biblioteca Mundi,* which was written by Vincent of Beauvais" (242). Barrette and Baldwin wonder why the *Tresor* enjoyed such great popularity "in the very twilight of such compendia, which after nearly a millennium of popularity in Latin were about to be abandoned completely." They explain the work's popularity and significance in terms of both its accessibility and its authority: "For the first time we see such a work written in a vernacular language; another key to the special popularity seems to be associated with Brunetto's skillfully organized plan [. . .], but the most compelling reason would have to be the venerable and unassailable authority of Brunetto's sources" (ix).

Arguably, the greatest contribution of *Li Livres dou Tresor* to both its own life world and to rhetorical history was that it, along with Latini's *La Rettorica,* offers the first vernacular version of classical rhetoric, in particular Cicero's *De Inventione,* written in Latin. And although Dante may have been disturbed by Latini's choice of a vernacular language (French instead of Italian), Latini's decision to write in the *lingua franca* of his day increased greatly the accessibility of his work, which was widely copied and distributed, not only in his native Italy, but also across the European continent. Latini himself was well aware of the importance of his decision to write in a French vernacular dialect, explaining in his introduction to the three-part *Tresor:* "If anyone asks why these books are written in romance, according to the French language, since I am an Italian, I shall say that there are two reasons, the first is that I am in France, and the second is that the French language is the most agreeable and most widespread among the nations" (2).

But beyond vernacularizing classical rhetoric for the first time, Latini offers, as Barrette and Baldwin suggest, a version of Cicero, especially, that is impressively comprehensive and accessible by virtue of its careful hierarchical organization. This organization, guided perhaps by Latini's use of "*alberi*," of organizational trees, evinces his profound appreciation of the canon of arrangement, for it is arrangement that seems to guide not only his presentation of the old, of what had already been said about rhetoric in classical sources, but also his invention of new commentary on, and applications of, what had been said, commentary and application directly influenced by present circumstances and personal ideology.

Although the *Tresor* is dedicated to a "handsome, gentle friend," a consideration of the work's contents (and of its advice) suggests that the actual audience is much broader than a single person. In their introduction to their translation, Barrette and Baldwin suggest that the audience consists of those who, like Cicero's audience, seek in eloquence, in language, a way to transcend their animal state. In addition to providing instruction in eloquence, however, it is Latini's purpose to provide knowledge that might speak to three informational needs he associates with his audience: "1) the nature of all things celestial and terrestrial; 2) the things a man should do and those he should not do; and 3) a rationale and proof of why a man should do some things and not do others" (x). These needs presuppose, of course, that human action, whether it is bodily or linguistic, needs to be informed by competence not only in rhetoric, but also by wisdom and goodness. At the heart of Latini's organizational plan, then, is a three-part philosophy of human action. And it is through such an ambitious plan that Latini evinces his sense (and the sense of his mentor, Cicero) that eloquence, and the rhetorical guidance of eloquence, needs to be grounded in a liberal education, ethical principles, and intelligent reasoning. In addition, Latini locates his philosophy of action within the city state, and in relationship to the republican governance of the city, and in so doing he establishes as his underlying audience not a single, "gentle friend," but the citizens of a democracy, including the *po-*

desta, who, by virtue of being factionally disinterested and elected from outside by the citizenry, governs not as an emperor, but as a representative of the people as a whole.

It is, then, with a sense of audience and political purpose that Latini organizes his compendious work, *Li Livres dou Tresor,* which is not only a rhetoric, but also an encyclopedia and a political treatise that offers advice to citizens of a constitutionally empowered democracy. Barrette and Baldwin provide the following hierarchy to account for Latini's three-part plan and his intention to treat theory (which I take to be knowledge relevant to governance), practice (which I take to be the guidance of governance), and logic (which I take to be the discourse of governance):

I. Theory ——— Theology Arithmetic
Physics Music
Mathematics ——— Geometry
Astronomy

II. Practice (which means how to govern)
    oneself = Ethics
    one's house = Economics
    a lordship = Politics ———
      Grammar: how to speak and write and read correctly
      Dialectic: how to prove our words [. . .] so that they seem to be proven and true
      Rhetoric: how to find, organize and say words which are good and full of wisdom

III. Logic ——— Dialectic, which teaches us to argue
    – Physic, which teaches us to prove the truth of our words

> – Sophistic, which teaches us "to prove a man's words to be true [. . .] by deceit and false reasons and sophisms and verisimilar arguments which have the outward appearance of truth, but in them there is no truth at all. (xi)

Barrette and Baldwin point out that, "while the above taxonomy is comprehensive, it is only partially carried out" in the *Tresor* itself (xi). Especially confusing are Parts II and III: Part II in fact focuses on Ethics, a subcategory of Practice, and Rhetoric, which is taxonomized as a subcategory of Politics (which in turn is a subcategory of Practice), becomes the focus of Part III (along with Politics), and Logic is treated as a subcategory of Rhetoric. Latini's reorganization of his initial taxonomy within the *Treso*r itself seems significant, for it repositions (and privileges) what might have been treated as a heading of the third degree—Rhetoric—as a heading of the first degree, a heading that is shared by Politics, which was initially envisioned as a heading of the second degree.

In short, it is Part III of *Li Livres dou Tresor* that becomes most important to rhetorical historians and theorists. In this Part's privileging of Rhetoric, and its paratactic association of Rhetoric with Politics, we read not only Latini's translation and application of Ciceronian rhetoric, but also his sense that such a rhetoric needs to work in partnership with republican ideology and political practice. Commenting on the relationship of Latini's rhetorical purposes and ideological motives to the title, organization, content, and style of the *Tresor,* Barrette and Baldwin write:

> The Treasure's purpose is clearly not intellectual, not intended as scholarly information for a scholarly public. One might be led to a certain conclusion from the very

choice of the image of the treasure, and the couching of everything in a remarkably plain and straightforward style, declaring that the achievement and improvement of one's status in the world is the most sublime of human aspirations; this statement reveals a point of view not philosophical but bourgeois, with a final goal which is economical, but in the final analysis political. (xii)

Indeed, in his decision to vernacularize classical rhetoric, in his association of rhetoric with republican (albeit bourgeois) ideology and with democratic practice, and in his focus on how rhetoric might guide not only speaking, but also writing, Latini emerged as an important and popular rhetorician during his own time. His story, and his treasure, most certainly deserve to be considered by those of us interested in the valuation and practice of persuasive discourse in the here and now, and in the context of democratic self-governance. Part III of *Li Livres dou Tresor,* especially, might speak to us urgently and helpfully as we endeavor to teach students to think and argue critically and well, and to resist the sort of imperial and oppressive discourse that Latini himself endeavored to resist.

Latini's Vernacularization and Application of Cicero

Before considering Latini's vernacularization and palimpsesting of his mentor, Cicero, in Part III of the *Tresor,* we might remember that Latini's impulse was to translate the work of Cicero as carefully as possible, but that his translation of Aristotle's conservative *Nicomachean Ethics* was a deliberate mistranslation, one that inverted Aristotle's hierarchy of desirable forms of government so that the last, a Timocracy, became the first; and the first, a Monarchy, became the last. Such mistranslation may seem to suggest a disregard for ethical practice on Latini's part, but from Latini's point of view, the rhetorical and political influence of Aristotle had been so great, and so complicit with the validation of empire, that his mistranslation in fact served to accomplish a greater good, the advancement of republican values and democratic approaches to the governance of the city state.

In fact, Latini's commitment to the Ciceronian emphasis on the necessity of the virtue of the rhetor, and on the importance of ethics, can be seen in Part II of the *Tresor,* in which Latini discusses the ethical aspects of both governance and rhetoric. Latini covers 132 topics having to do with ethics These topics comprehend matters treated by Aristotle in his own *Nicomachean Ethics.* Latini includes "Courage," "Generosity," and "Constancy," but he focuses on notions of "Moral and Intellectual Virtue" (including sub-topics such as "Prudence," "Temperance," and "Courage") and "Justice" (including sub-topics such as "Rigor" and "Liberality"). Topics such as "The person to whom you are speaking," "Why you speak," "How you speak," and "Being careful about the time to speak" link Latini's discussion of ethics to classical rhetorical notions of audience, purpose, decorum, and *kairos.* However, the rhetorical notion of "ethos" seems to be at the heart of Part II, for Latini, like his mentor Cicero, believed that rhetorical effectiveness must be grounded in the knowledge and goodness of the rhetor, a belief that is foregrounded in his discussion of "What one must be careful to do before speaking," which has to do with, "First of all, who you are who wish to speak."

The progression of the three parts of Latini's *Treso*r suggests that it is a treasure not because of its comprehensive treatment of the "scientific" knowledge of its time and of its

The Currency of Latini's Rhetorical Treasure

aggregation of Biblical and classical sources (altogether, 437 topics are covered); instead, it might be a treasure in its recommendation and advancement of a kind of sequenced and value-laden curriculum. This curriculum begins with the acquisition of "knowledge"; it then moves on to an examination of "ethics" before it concludes by providing rhetorical and political advice. In other words, it is a curriculum that asserts the importance of knowing much and living ethically to the quality of the discourse of a democratically constituted city state. Such a categorically sequenced curriculum might be seen as problematical to those of us who have been influenced by social-constructivist assumptions concerning epistemology and discourse, but like any sequenced process (including the five canons of rhetoric), it has systemic and recursive potential. Indeed, it was through (and in) intertextual and social discourse, inevitably ideological and value-laden, that Latini constructed his treasure—perhaps, in fact, the result of oral lectures that were copied down by students. And it is contemporary theoretical and pedagogical discourse that, even in its rejection of linear processes and rigid categories, might find in Latini's *Tresor* not only what seems to be some sort of foundational, sequenced, and taxonomic curriculum, but also intertextual resonances having to do with the valuation of knowing and being in relationship to saying and doing. If this is so, then contemporary compositionists in America might find a kind of soul mate in Latini—especially in terms of his profound understanding of the inevitable relationship between ideology and discourse and in his advocacy of what might be called, today, "liberatory" approaches to both literacy and education.

I turn, now, to Part III of *Li Livres dou Tresor*, in which Latini provides for us not only a version of classical rhetoric that might seem familiar, but also a historically contextualized and politically motivated supplement to and application of that rhetoric. From the beginning, Latini's indebtedness to Cicero is clear, for it is Cicero who is most frequently summarized and paraphrased, and upon whose translated work Latini's own Rhetoric is palimpsested. As translator of Cicero, Latini summarizes: "Cicero says that the most important science relative to governing the city is rhetoric, that is to say, the science of speaking, for if there were no speech, there would be no city, nor would there be any establishment of justice or human company, and although speech is given to all men, Cato says wisdom is given to few." He writes over his summary with an interesting supplement:

> For this reason, I say that speakers are of four types, for some are endowed with great sense and eloquence, and this is the cream of the crop; others are devoid of both eloquence and sense, and this is a great misfortune; others are devoid of sense, but they speak too well, and this is a very great peril; others are full of sense, but they remain silent because of the poverty of their speech, and so they need help. (279)

In his supplement of Cicero, I read the ideology of Latini the republican and the heart of Latini the teacher. His impulse, it seems, is to "help" those who have sense, but who lack eloquence." Latini's "Rhetoric," then, seems to have much to do with both instruction and empowerment, with giving voice to those who "remain silent because of the poverty of their speech."

But Latini also draws from other classical sources, including Aristotle and the sophists. At times his *Tresor* affirms the value of his diverse sources; at other times it enters into debate with them. Never, though, does Latini challenge the wisdom of Cicero, his ideological and rhetorical mentor. And rarely does Latini directly challenge Aristotle, even though he deliberately mistranslates his conservative take on governance. Here is Latini's discussion of "Rhetoric, what it is, its function and its goal":

> Rhetoric is a science which teaches us fully and perfectly to express ourselves in public and private matters, and its whole purpose is to say words in such a way that those who hear the words will believe them. You should know that rhetoric comes under the science of governing a city, according to what Aristotle says in his book, which is translated above into romance, just as the art of making bridles and saddles is under the art of chivalry. The function of this art, according to Cicero, is to speak thoughtfully in such a way as to make others believe what we say. Between the function and the goal there is this difference: in the function the speaker is concerned with the goal, that is, he speaks in such a way that he will be believed; and in the goal he considers what is appropriate to the function, that is, to have others believe him through his speaking. Illustration: the function of the doctor is to practice medicine thoughtfully in order to heal, and his goal is to heal through his medicine, and quickly. The function of rhetoric is to speak thoughtfully according to the instruction of the art, and its goal is the reason for which he is speaking. The material of rhetoric is what the speaker speaks about, just as sick people are the material of the doctor. About this Gorgias says that all things which are appropriate to speak about are the mate-

rial of this art. Hermagoras says that this material is in causes and in questions; he says that causes are disputes over specific people or specific things, and in this respect he was not speaking error; but he said that questions are disputes which do not specify the people or the circumstances, such as the size of the sun or the stability of the firmament; in this respect he was mistaken, for this material has nothing to do with governing a city: it is rather the proper domain of philosophers who devote themselves to profound learning. For this reason those people are mistaken who believe that telling fables or ancient stories or whatever else one might say is material for rhetoric. But what one says with one's mouth or sends in thoughtful letters for the purpose of persuading others to believe, or disputing, praising, condemning or taking counsel with respect to a given matter, or to something which requires a judgment: all this is material for rhetoric. But everything which one does not say artfully, that is, by noble words, serious and full of meaning, or which does not deal with any of the above-mentioned matters, is outside of this science and far from its rules. For this reason Aristotle says that the material of this art is concerned with three things alone, that is, demonstration, counsel, and judgment. (279–280)

I provide the above passage in its entirety to show how Latini uses classical sources to advance his own argument: that rhetoric is a science that comprehends ceremonial, forensic, and deliberative argumentation in relationship to the "governing of a city." Too, it suggests Latini's attraction to the political, substantive, and stylistic proclivities of Cicero, and his subordination of Aristotelian and sophistic notions of rhetoric to the problems and concerns of democratic debate and governance.

Much of Part III of Latini's *Tresor*—including his treatment of the five canons of rhetoric, "*stasis*" theory, invention, and deductive argumentation—covers classical rhetorical ground already familiar to American rhetoricians and teachers of writing. And his emphasis on the Ciceronian, six-part approach to arrangement is equally familiar. However, what is novel, and worthy of notice, is the way Latini palimpsests his own version of rhetoric on top of Cicero's, and the way he provides extensive and specific advice concerning the canon of arrangement. In fact, it is the kind of organizational guidance that originally interested Corax and later Cicero that dominates the discussion of rhetoric in Part III. This guidance is organized taxonomically—we can see Latini's *alberi* at work again—on the basis of the six parts recommended by Cicero and then double-translated (from Latin to French and from French to English): "the Prologue," "the Narrative," "Partition," "Confirmation," "Refutation," and "Conclusion." Latini's subdivision of these structural categories is impressive. Of 72 topics concerning rhetoric, over 50 have to do with an audience-sensitive consideration of aspects of effectively arranging persuasive discourse.

It is impossible to discuss all of Latini's rhetorical topics; thus, I recommend that American rhetoricians read the translation of *Li Livres dou Treso*r in its entirety, focusing on Part III. However, I will quote at length one of Latini's subtopics having to do with arrangement in order to provide the overall flavor of Part III and to illustrate its detailed attention to persuasive praxis. Here is what he has to say about "The sixth branch of the narrative, that is, the conclusion, which is the last":

> After the instruction on refutation and all of the first five branches of the narrative, the last one comes, that is, the conclusion, where the speaker concludes his reasons and through this brings his narrative to an end. However, we find that Hermagoras said in his books that before the conclusion there must be a digression, and thus he gave seven branches to the narrative. But the very wise Tullius Cicero, who surpasses all men in good speaking, severely criticizes Hermagoras' judgment. You clearly heard above that a digression is when a speaker departs somewhat from his own matter and goes to another, in order to praise himself or his position, or to criticize his adversary and his position, or to confirm not through arguments but by promoting his cause, according to what the master said above in the chapter on how one can promote one's cause or one's subject matter in many other places. With respect to this digression, Cicero says that it is not and must not be a separate branch of the narrative. For this reason the master [Latini insofar as he speaks for Cicero] will now be silent and will say only that the conclusion is the exit and the end of the narrative, but it is subject to the arguments of the branches of the narrative. And you should know that the conclusion has three parts, and these are recapitulation, disdain, and pity, and you will now hear about each one separately and in detail, beginning with recapitulation. (343)

The Currency of Latini's Rhetorical Treasure

In this passage, one reads Latini's drive toward providing practical rhetorical advice in great detail and also his drive toward organizing that advice hierarchically. Especially interesting, however, is the way he privileges Cicero's advice again and works to discredit classical sources he believes to be problematic. As a result, argumentation and decorum emerge as having more rhetorical value than praise of self or *ad hominem* attack, which Latini sees as ineffective digression. Indeed, Latini follows his own advice, choosing to "be silent" rather than developing a digression of his own. And yet, despite his effort to avoid digression, he shows "disdain" for Hermagoras (by evoking the greater authority of Cicero) and engenders "pity" for himself (insofar as he speaks not for himself, but for Cicero).

Guided by Latini, and writing as his student, I conclude this section of my own third chapter by "recapitulating": it is Latini's effort to link, in *Li Livres dou Tresor,* his rhetorical advice with knowledge and ethical practice that not only gives new, vernacular breath and voice to Cicero, but that also results in a comprehensive and critical Rhetoric, one that is particularly sensitive to the problem of democratic governance. In the second section of Part III, a section that focuses on politics, Latini applies his encyclopedia, his ethics, and his rhetoric to political praxis. Thus, the Tresor concludes by considering political matters having to do with knowledge of the natural biological order and medieval philosophy ("The comparison between the blessings of the body and of fortune"); with ethical deliberation ("The quarrel between honesty and profit"); and with the rhetoric and discourse, both spoken and written, through which democracy is constituted and practiced ("The form of the letter" and "What the lord must do when he receives the letter"). Alas, I am digressing, but perhaps my conclusion is sufficient to show why it is we need to hold in "disdain" those rhetorics devoid of intellectual, moral, and political value, and why we need to "pity" a great teacher and rhetorician, damned by his own student, but the giver of a remarkable treasure. And now I will be silent. For a while.

Latini's Contributions to the Ars Dictaminis and the Rhetoric of Writing

At this point in my search for Latini, I have been unable to find an article focusing on his significance as a rhetorician and teacher in mainstream American journals having to do with rhetoric or composition. And there is very little in the literature pertaining to Latini that considers, in detail, his application of Ciceronian rhetorical and ethical implications for writing. This is unfortunate, considering Latini's many comments about writing. As Holloway notes in her comprehensive Latini bibliography (*Brunetto Latini: An Analytic Bibliography*): "Brunetto Latini believed that writing was both a political and ethical practice" (63).

Ironically, the one American article I could find that treats the implications of Latini's work for writing appeared, in 1968, in *The Quarterly Journal of Speech*. In "Brunetto Latini's Rhetoric of Letter Writing," James East considers how Latini's work participated in the evolving *ars dictaminis* of his day. East notes that, in Part III of his *Tresor*, Latini "combines the principles of Ciceronian rhetoric on the art of speaking and the medieval rhetoric of letter writing," resulting in "a rhetoric that is applicable to both oral and written discourse" (241). The *ars dictaminis,* East explains, "which had been a subordinate part of rhetoric in the early Middle Ages, became an independent branch of learning in some universities, especially those which stressed the study of the law." He adds, "In some places it usurped the whole field of rhetoric and was called *rhetorica*," a "type of rhetoric" that was "a separate branch of instruction," originating in Italy and fully developed "at the University of Bologna, which excelled in the study of law" (245).

The Currency of Latini's Rhetorical Treasure

As East argues, Latini's particular contribution to the *ars dictaminis* lies in his translation and application of Cicero's *De Inventione,* for it is from Cicero that Latini takes advice concerning the arrangement of spoken discourse, which he then applies to the writing of public discourse in the form of letters. Although East gestures at Latini's "preoccupation with the structure of discourse" (244), he goes on to show that this preoccupation was subordinated to sensitivity to audience and to the specific writing context. Thus, Latini does not recommend a rigid application of the Ciceronian six-part arrangement structure, but a flexible and writing-related version. One might wonder how the canon of arrangement, originally developed to help political orators, might be imported to the *ars dictaminis*. After reflecting on Latini's own assertion that the principles of oral persuasion and letter writing "are the same because it cannot matter whether one commits an account to word or to a letter," East argues that it is Latini's sense of the focus and scope of rhetoric that makes possible the conflation of advice about speaking and advice about writing. For Latini, the focus of rhetoric needs to be on "controversy," and its range needs to comprehend controversies arising "not only in courts, but in all remarks regarding counsel, entreaty, or written communication" (243). The Ciceronian approach to arrangement, then, in its anticipation of audience resistance whenever and wherever controversial matters are being argued, is seen and used by Latini as a psychology of persuasion, one that anticipates the concerns of a resisting audience and that pragmatically speaks (or writes) to those needs as they might arise in sequence.

East notices that a "major section" of Latini's rhetoric "is a comparison of the parts of a Ciceronian oration with the parts of a letter." East writes: "Latini says the differences between the two are in appearance only." He explains that what letter writers call salutation Cicero includes under prologue, what Cicero calls partition the letter writers include under narration, and what Cicero calls confirmation and refutation the letter writers include under petition" (243).

East provides the following diagram to clarify how Latini applied to the composition of a letter the arrangement strategy that Cicero recommends for oration:

Oration	Letter
prologue	salutation
narration	prologue
partition	narration
confirmation	petition
refutation	conclusion (243)
conclusion	

Latini's discussion of letter writing, then, can be seen as a palimpsest on *De Inventione,* one that preserves the spirit and much of the letter of Cicero's treatment of arrangement, but one that also shows how that treatment might be adjusted to the particular requirements of writing to an audience that is not present.

In my view, it is Latini's flexible application of Cicero to the *ars dictaminis* of his day, and his keen understanding of the special demands of writing, that best argues his great relevance to those of us who endeavor to apply classical rhetoric to our own writing and teaching of writing. From a structuralist perspective, we can see Latini articulating "surface" versions of an "underlying" rhetoric, understanding not only the "deep structure" of persuasive arrangement, but also how that deep, abstract structure might be "transformed" in rhetorics sensitive to both immediate contexts and different technologies of delivery.

Latini is clearly sensitive to the special demands of writing, in which the audience must be imagined. In "The two ways of speaking, by mouth or by writing, and on what topics," he observes of the letter writer:

The Currency of Latini's Rhetorical Treasure

> He knows very well that the one to whom he is sending letters will object to what he is letting him know, and for this reason, the wise writer strengthens his letters with beautiful and good reasons and with strong arguments which support what he wants, just as if the dispute were face-to-face. Such letters pertain to rhetoric, just as the song does which one lover uses to speak to the other. From this one can understand that there can be two types of dispute, either open, when one defends oneself against the other orally or in writing, or not open, when one sends letters filled with good arguments against the defense one thinks the other has. (284)

Moreover, Latini values writing letters as a way of communicating to a newly elected official the responsibilities that the political position entails and securing the official's agreement to perform the position according to the will of the people. In the second section of Part III of the *Tresor*, a section devoted to politics and governance, Latini instructs "In what way the lord should be elected":

> When the wise men of the city who are charged with the election are in agreement about a good man, they must immediately consider the practice and the laws and the customs of the city, and according to these things they must elect their magistrate in the name of the one who gives all honor and good things. They must immediately draw up letters, well and wisely, and inform the good man of how they have elected him and determined that he will be lord and magistrate of their land the following year, and inform him briefly of the extent of his

duties, and clarify all the details at the outset so that no misunderstanding might arise. For this they must specifically inform him of the day when he must be physically present in their city and take his oath to the constitution, and that he should bring with him judges, and notaries, and other officials to do these and other things, and how many days he must stay after the end to give an account of whatever people might wish to ask him about, and what salary he must have, how it should be paid, and the number of horses he must bring with him; and that all dangers to himself and to his property will be his responsibility. He must be informed of these covenants and others connected to this undertaking in writing, according to the practice and law of the city. (354-55)

In the topic that immediately follows, "The form of the letter," Latini offers an example of the sort of letter that should be given to an elected official. Then, in "The things the lord must do when he receives the letters," Latini suggests the use and disposition of the letters once the official has received them:

In this way or in some other which the wise writer chooses, these letters will be sent to the lord, with the complete charter of the agreements, and the messenger carrying them will give them to him courteously and in private, without hue and cry. The lord must take them in the manner of a wise man and go quietly to a private place, and break the seal and look at the letters and learn what is in them, and mull over with great care what he must do, and seek out the counsel of his good friends, and ascertain if he has the qualifications of such an undertaking. (357)

One can read in the excerpts above Brunetto Latini's strong belief in the value of writing as a means of ensuring contractual and constitutional understandings. Moreover, he seems to understand that writing, as opposed to speaking, can provide the kind of detachment and reflection that might facilitate the negotiation of both power and responsibility, the sort of negotiation that is vitally important to the overall discourse and success of democratic governance. And even though Latini attempts to minimize the differences between speaking and writing, it is possible to find, in his *Tresor,* the beginnings of a rhetoric that might be applied specifically to writing and an acknowledgment of the unique benefits of writing.

However, it is also possible to find in Part III of Latini's *Tresor* a problematizing impulse, one that resonates with contemporary notions of textual ambiguity and instability. In "The dispute which arises from the written text," Latini observes:

> The dispute through written words can be in five ways: for sometimes the word does not agree with the meaning of the person writing, and at other times it happens that two words or two laws or several disagree with one another, and sometimes it seems that what is written means two things or several, and at other times it seems that what is written presents meaning and examples which are appropriate to something else which is not written down yet, and sometimes the dispute hinges on knowing what the force of a written word is, so as to know what it is supposed to mean. (285)

The above discussion, in its focus on the pragmatic and semantic dislocation of writing from speech (and from immediate contextual reference), sounds almost postmodern. And, indeed, Latini's sophisticated and complicated notions of textuality suggest that he is, in a way, "one of us," not only a teacher of rhetoric, but also a teacher of writing. Surely we can at least find Latini, for now, by examining our own contemporary impulses as theorists and as practicing teachers, for he seems to be mirrored in us, and we in him, in remarkable ways.

A Rhetorician for the Here and Now

As I near the end of the first stage of my pilgrimage, a more or less sedentary search for Latini among textual sources acquired mainly through interlibrary loan, I understand that I have not found him completely, for I have not yet experienced how my search will change my teaching following my anticipated return journey to Florence. Indeed, I am at this point more a student than a teacher, studying through the texts of Holloway and others translations of the texts of Latini, and through Latini, translations of the texts of Cicero—layers upon layers of texts, palimpsests on top of palimpsests. And I find myself still at the outer layers, still lost without the guidance of other scholars, better scholars. I am not nearly the student that Dante was, and my own writing seems, in retrospect, hopelessly superficial, my own pilgrimage tale a pathetic imitation of Dante's great allegory. Yet, unlike Dante, I refuse to find the mentor from whom I endeavor to learn condemned to run forever in the Seventh Circle of Hell. I find myself becoming increasingly appreciative of Latini's rhetorical vision, perhaps because, in my own case, I am deeply sympathetic to his political and intellectual liberalism, his aversion to institutionalized structures of oppressive power and control. I realize that my own tale so far, like any tale, runs the risk of mythologizing

The Currency of Latini's Rhetorical Treasure

its hero, of seeing my mentor not as he was, but as I would have him be. Perhaps such mythologizing is inevitable; perhaps in all of our versions of the past we see what we need to see. I know with certainty that, for a variety of reasons, I need to see Latini as a figure who might still speak to me, speak to my own community of rhetoricians and writing teachers, not as a dead and obscure teacher, but as a living and present voice. I choose, therefore, to continue searching, hoping that in my return visit to Florence, and in my conversation with Julia Bolton Holloway, I will find Latini, if not in Paradise, at least in the context of my own experience as a traveler and as a teacher.

But at this point in my pilgrimage, having traveled textually, at least, I find that my role has shifted some. I feel an urgency, before continuing, to become a kind of importer of Latini's work and legacy, and the discourse of important Latini scholars, to the rhetorical canon that has been constructed by American theorists and teachers of writing. This urgency has to do with my sympathy for Latini's obscurity, especially in my own research and teaching community. I wonder, now, how is it that the teacher of Dante, the first vernacularizer of Aristotle and Cicero, and a great advocate of liberatory approaches to political discourse, could have been so neglected. It is clear to me that our neglect needs to be addressed, and at the close of this, the first part of my own Book, I will endeavor to argue for Latini's inclusion in our rhetorical canon. He deserves to be included and widely read, as do the Latini scholars who have already recognized his value and his contemporary significance.

Like Latini and like Dante, I have experienced a sense of exile in my search thus far, in my own case an exile from my home community of scholars and teachers. Indeed, not a single person in my department, and very few people across my campus, had ever head of Latini until I started my search and, like the Ancient Mariner, began stopping every third person to tell the story of Latini. Like me before my conversation with Max, my colleagues and my journals had little or nothing to say about the teacher of Dante. And thus my pilgrimage, to this point, has led me away from my department, away from my university, away from my discipline, and away from my country. I am, indeed, in exile from my ordinary world of scholarship and teaching.

It is from figurative exile, then, that I write home to American rhetoricians and writing teachers. And before traveling any further, I will endeavor to provide what I believe are compelling reasons for our recognition of Brunetto Latini, for exhuming both his biography and his *Tresor* from their obscure burial places in archives and libraries across the oceans of our neglect. Instructed by my mentor, Brunetto, I will present these reasons in a modest hierarchy of my own making, his *alberi* very much on my mind as I do so.

Reasons for Recognizing and Reading Latini

Historical
    Teacher of Dante
    Vernacularizer of Aristotle and Cicero
    Participant in significant public rhetoric of his day
    Widely read poet and rhetorician during his day

Rhetorical
    Developer of *Epistolarium* and *ars dictaminis*
    Contributor to forensic, deliberative, and negotiatory approaches to rhetoric
    Popularizer and explicator of Cicero
    Advocate of the importance of broad knowledge and ethics to rhetorical praxis
    Advocate of the importance of rhetoric to democratic governance
    Explicator and developer of the canon of arrangement

Developer of strategies for hierarchical organization
Visionary with postmodern notions of language and intertextuality

Pedagogical
Advocate of vernacular and inclusive literacies
Teacher with liberatory impulses
Teacher of both rhetoric and writing

Before moving beyond my textual search for Latini, and beginning my journey to Florence, I offer one last reason for American rhetoricians and writing teachers to recognize and read Latini: he indirectly contributed to documents that underlie American political identity and practice. Noticing with Lascito Davidsohn the remarkable resemblance of Latini's work to the American Constitution and the Declaration of Independence, Holloway, in *Twice-Told Tales,* asserts that "this likeness is more than just a matter of style," indeed that "it is combined theory and *praxis,* in literature and history." She adds, "An American President, swearing upon the book, taking office for a limited term, is a latter day Florentine podesta" (303). Insofar as American teachers of rhetoric and writing are concerned with our students' critical participation in democratic literacy and discourse, we need to look to Latini not only as a historical influence on such literacy and discourse, but also as one who has much to teach us in the here and now.

Part II: Toward an Open Book of My Own

4 On Foot in Florence

It is difficult to know what to do when moving from one component of a Book to another, from the *Purgatorio*, say, to the *Paradiso*. As Latini taught Dante, hierarchy and headings help. But in my own case, this movement seems especially complicated since the ways of knowing in the two components of my Book are so very different. I am moving, now, from texts and reading to experience and observation, from a way of knowing that depends so much on seeing the word to one that depends on both seeing and listening. This movement is an important part of my pilgrimage, my search for Latini, for it will help me to ground myself in cultural context and to understand, better, Latini's significance in terms of places and voices. The problem with this movement, these steps that lead me from a realm of reading to one of feeling, is twofold:

1. My steps are not steps, but, instead, a trans-Atlantic flight that, in a sleep-depriving way, takes me rapidly to the context I seek and a time-frame that is seven hours ahead of my normal one. I arrive the morning following the afternoon upon which I departed. Indeed, it feels like the "dream vision" component of my pilgrimage begins just now, begins upon arrival in Italy.

2. The context in which I find myself is not the same historical context in which Latini lived and wrote. As my daughter tells me, following the Risorgimento of

the nineteenth century, when Italy became a unified nation, Florence and other Italian cities changed dramatically, its political identity as a city increasingly complicated by national and international events and affiliations.

I will walk the same streets that Latini walked, but the streets have become something else—stony traces of the past, true, but traces that now lead outward from the city's center to the Autostrada del Sole Milano-Roma, the Santa Maria Novella Train Station, and the Amerigo Vespucci Airport.

Illumination 1: A stony trace of the past.

Because I am now entering the experiential component of my Book, entering a component that is more decidedly a travel narrative, a literal pilgrimage, I decide to take digital photographs, hoping I will find a way to work them into the writing. This decision seems right, seems in keeping with the medieval predisposition toward textual illuminations. Latini, I believe, would have found my impulse to embed in my Book photographs, electronic illuminations, acceptable, perhaps even desirable.

And now I must resume somewhere—in the middle of things, most certainly—and I must continue to write if I am to find Latini within the boundaries (and distortions) of my own Book. So—I am here, in my daughter's apartment, my exile from my home community of teachers and scholars more deeply felt, more obvious. But I am also with my daughter, who has become as much Italian as American during these past fifteen years, and who does not see her condition as one of exile. No, she tells me, she chooses to be here, more of an immigrant than an exile. In a sense, then, I have come home, to the most significant member of my family, to a place that my daughter has chosen in which to work, live, and speak. And, thus, I gain another guide, another teacher: "*mia figlia*" (my daughter), as I deeply know, "*e mia insegnante*" (is my teacher). What better result for a pilgrim journey than to rediscover one's own daughter, not as a child, but as a teacher and as an informant.

During the days, as my daughter works, I visit, in an almost ritualistic way, my favorite places in Florence (the Duomo, Santa Croce, the Uffizi, Santo Spirito, and so forth)—and also the little towns of Tuscany that I love (Fiesole, Lucca, Siena, Arezzo, and Pistoia). But this trip I am searching for Latini, and the landscape seems entirely different, suddenly informed by thousands of years of political history, inhabited by the ghosts of Etruscans and Romans, haunted by the teacher of Dante. My focus in Florence has shifted from art to political discourse and rhetoric, from architectural monuments to social *comune*. I gaze, still, at the Duomo, amazed by its size and beauty, but now my gaze includes the ubiquitous graffiti on neighboring buildings, construction barricades, and sidewalks, much of it urging for "*Pace*" (Peace) or criticizing American involvement in Iraq. The graffiti, I notice, is almost inevitably political here. It has little to do with gangs, sex, love affairs, or people's names. The graffiti of the Comune of Florence focuses on political parties, ideological affiliations, world affairs, and social problems. It is a display of deliberative assertions; it is a lively and intertextual display of political rhetoric; it is the deeply vernacular voice of the commune.

Much of the graffiti has an epigrammatic quality, a poetic quality. On a construction barricade protecting restoration of the exterior of the Duomo, I read:

Illumination 2: A street poem for peace.

Facciamo L'Ammmore
Non Facciamo La Guerra
Vogliamo La Pace
Su Tutta La Terra.
(Make love, not war. Wish for peace on all the earth.)

In the same way that medieval Florentine poetry participated in the deliberative rhetoric of its time, this graffiti, an urgent message of protest, evinces a sense of *kairos* and exigence, its rhyming association of war with earth available not only to Italians, but also American tourists who cluster near the Duomo. I am touched by the stuttering inclusion of extra "m's" in *"Amore"*: they add weight and emphasis to the key word, the word that is at the heart of *The Divine Commedy*. But I am also saddened by the transience of the text. When the restoration is complete, the boards of the barricade will be torn down, its palimpsesting message destroyed like parchment in fire. I photograph the poem digitally, hoping to serve as a kind of twenty-first-century copyist, hoping that my copy might save both the form and the force of the poem.

It strikes me that it is in the graffiti, not in the great churches and monuments and sculptures, that I find, at last, the voice and the spirit I seek: a voice, like Latini's voice, that is written underneath and in spite of discourses of power and wealth; it is a voice that is part of an urgent discourse having to do with the interests of the people. Near Santa Croce, a monument to the art and discourse of Renaissance Florence, the great Franciscan edifice that contains the tombs of figures as influential (and diverse) as Michelangelo, Machiavelli, and Galileo, I read, spray-painted on the wall of a building, "Meno chiese; piu case!" "Fewer churches, more houses"—the statement seems more urgent, more volatile because of its proximity to Santa Croce. Although I cannot imagine Florence without Santa Croce, especially, I understand that the graffiti speaks at the margins of a memorializing discourse, a romanticizing discourse. And while Latini's discourse and teaching was not advanced through graffiti, it was said and done in ways that were decidedly public and political.

As the days pass, the graffiti affects me. "Latini lives!" I want to spray paint on the walls of the *Sottopassaggio* near my daughter's apartment, a concrete underpass for those on foot and bicycle that is nearly covered with graffiti, a sort of underground library of political texts and colorful illuminations.

Illumination 3: Graffiti in the *Sottopassaggio*.

But I doubt that my little intertextual comment would be noticed, and I don't have the necessary paint. The graffiti reminds me, though, that I need to make another ritualistic trip, one that I make every time I come to Florence, to see a little bit of graffiti that was done during the Renaissance, not in words, but as a sort of caricature. At least this was what I was told by Domenico, an artist and friend of my daughter, during a prior visit. "See," he told me as we stared

Illumination 4: *Sottopassaggio* graffiti aimed at speakers of English.

at a small cartoon-like profile carved into stone in the wall of a building near the Piazza Della Signoria, "This is Savaronola. Michelangelo did this himself!" I wanted to believe him then, as I do still. Graffiti making fun of the repressive monk who gained power during the Renaissance and who was an enemy of art—graffiti mocking and resisting a force of repression and control. I walk to the Piazza Della Signoria and then search wall after wall, hoping to see again the image that I cannot find at first, an image that, I begin to fear, I dreamed—or worse, an image that once existed, but that has now been erased by city officials. But at last I find it: it is still there, still missing the kind of explanatory signage that accompanies almost all public art in Florence.

This time, as I gaze at the image, I think not of Michelangelo, but of Latini, remembering his ironic and mocking letter to the Pavian Ghibellines after the murder of the Abbott Tesauro of Vallombrosa. This, I realize as I gaze at the gazing caricature, is the graffiti of resistance, a kind of speech act that intends to subvert privileged and powerful discourse.

Michael Kleine

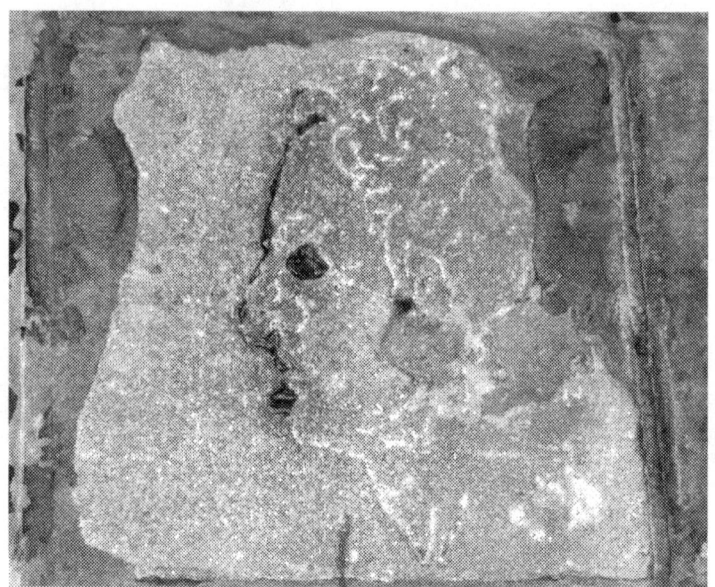

Illumination 5: Michelangelo's caricature of Savaronola?

My sense of seeing seems focused in a very different way as I search for Latini. I seek out, more and more, glimpses of Florence having to do with its political and rhetorical heritage. In the Uffizi, I am drawn to the bust of Cicero. It is placed among the busts of other famous Romans in one of the long, sunlit halls that connect the various galleries of the museum.

During prior trips to Florence, I had wandered from gallery to gallery, gazing at the spectacular paintings, but this time I am drawn to the busts, and I find Cicero, the great advocate of Republican democracy. "Latini's teacher," I muse, "living on less in this bust than in his rhetorical legacy."

I return to Santa Maggiore to see the memorial column from the tomb of Brunetto Latini.

Illumination 6: Bust of Cicero.

This time I understand the column's significance, evoking as it does Latini's sense of Cicero, who seemed to Latini both a strong column and an unstagnant fountain. How fitting that the most conspicuous memorial to Latini evokes not only Latini, but also Latini's greatest classical influence. The church is deserted, and in its profound silence I hear and read Latini's obscurity. That same day I walk over to the Bargello, hoping to see Giotto's fresco of Dante, the fresco in which Latini appears, almost like an apparition, at Dante's side. But, alas, the Magdalene Chapel is closed, undergoing restoration. It suffices that I know, now, that he is in there—frozen in time next to his famous student, Dante. And then I wander along the Arno toward Santa Croce, knowing I will see again the huge statue of Dante.

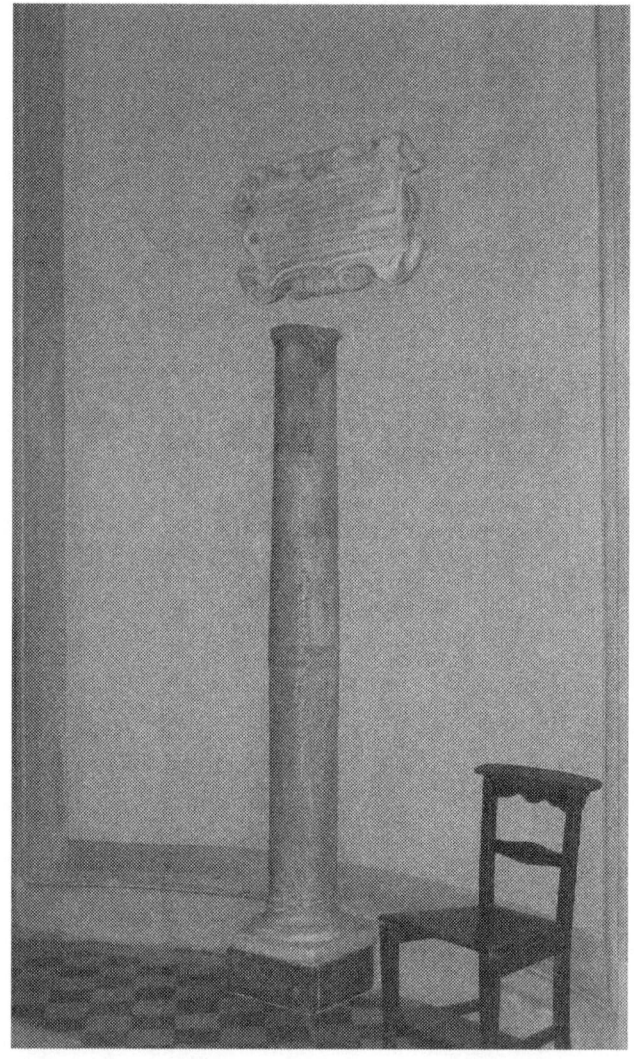

Illumination 7: Column from Latini's tomb, an obscure memorial.

It is the contrast between the great Dante memorial and the hidden-away memorial to Latini that most moves me as a teacher. The student magnified, the teacher remembered

Illumination 8: Statue of Dante, next to Santa Croce.

in the shadows of a relatively unknown church, literal place of Latini's "burial," which tourists hurry past on their way from the train station to the Duomo and to Santa Croce.

This is as it should be for teachers of writing, this is what we most desire, and yet, as an obscure teacher searching for another obscure teacher, I am not completely satisfied.

Illumination 9: Santa Maggiore, literal place of Latini's "burial."

I search for a memorial to Latini that seems appropriate. In a week, I will interview Julia Bolton Holloway at the Gatehouse of the English Cemetery, and I know I will see, there, copies of Latini's manuscripts—the greatest memorials of all—and yet, for the time being, I wander the streets of Florence in a ritualistic sort of way, returning to what I have seen before, hoping to see, and to feel, something new. And then, one evening, during a walk near my daughter's apartment, I diverge from the known streets, the known routes, and I experience something very strange: the setting sun is pulling me toward unknown territory. I fear that I have become lost, have in fact found the originating condition, the originating feeling, that Dante experienced in the *Inferno*. The evening light rubricates the narrow street down which I walk, and I pass in and out of shadows. I am, quite literally, lost. Terrified, I glance upward in hopes of seeing, inscribed on a building near an intersection, the name of the street that is taking me to an unknown destination. I experience, just then, the closest to an epiphany that I have ever had known. The unknown street is named, indeed; it is the Via Latini. "I'll be damned," I mutter to myself, at once aware of the irony of this muttering. "A Via, a Way, that is named after the teacher for whom I search."

Illumination 10: Off the beaten track, on the Via Brunetto Latini.

I pull my torn map of Florence from my jacket pocket, searching to find this street in the waning light, hoping to see it mapped. I cannot find it at first, my eyes scanning back and forth over the representation of the maze of Florence's streets. Finally, though, I find it—in very small print—and I understand where I have come, and how I must go home.

Perfect, it seems, that the Florentine street named for Latini is represented on my map as a small street, an obscure street. And perfect that it is, at least, represented. I turn around on the Via Latini, oriented now and eager to return to my daughter's apartment, to share my find with her. But my gaze has been turned upward, and I see, now, banners hanging from the windows of second-story apartments. There are two of them, nearly side by side: the first reads "Pace" and the second reads "No Alla Guerra."

Illumination 11: Peace banner on the Via Brunetto Latini.

Illumination 12: Banner urging for no more war on the Via Brunetto Latini.

The voices of peace abound in this great city, echoing and palimpsesting old treaties, old negotiations.

I feel, suddenly, at home. I feel comforted. Here, on the Via Latini, I find the written voices that resonate most with Latini's significance. They are, of course, vernacular voices, popular voices. They are voices that speak through graffiti and on banners. They are the voices I pray my students will discover, writing to resist what is unjust, writing to promote the kind of love that Paulo Freire urges. If I were to write a *Divine Commedy,* I would want these voices to join the voices of Cicero, Latini, and Freire in a final canto of liberation, light, and love.

5 The Illuminating Presence of Julia Bolton Holloway

There is a November chill in the air, desiccated leaves falling and swirling, as my daughter and I stroll toward the Piazzale Dontatello, where the English Cemetery is located. Julia Holloway, who has been the principal guide during my search for Latini, is the Curator there and lives in the Gatehouse.

Illumination 13: Gatehouse of the English Cemetery.

It seems appropriate to my daughter and me that Julia, whose scholarship has comprehended some of the figures buried in the English Cemetery (including Elizabeth Barrett Browning), now lives and works in proximity to the graves of others who were English, who once wrote Books, and who loved Florence as Holloway loves Florence. I am carrying a little tray piled high with "dolci," with desert pastries we will contribute to the meal to which Julia has invited us both. My daughter, who leads me to this place of the dead and this place where a living and important scholar now works, suggested the offering, which the proprietor of a small neighborhood bakery assembled, wrapped, and tied up with a bow. We arrive at the gate to the cemetery at seven, the agreed upon time, but the cemetery seems dark, the marble tombs reflecting the headlights of passing cars, no perceptible light shining from the nearly windowless gatehouse. My daughter rings the bell, and almost immediately the gate swings open. A woman emerges from the shadows by the door of the house, smiling and welcoming us immediately. Her head is covered by a scarf. Even in the darkness Amy and I can see her smile and her warm eyes. Both of us (we agree later) feel an instant sense of warmth and connection. "Welcome, Amy and Michael," she says, remembering our names from my emails and a prior telephone conversation. "Please do come in."

"In" is the kitchen of the gatehouse, somewhat dim, but warm and filled with the smell of a leek soup Julia is preparing. Helping her is Assunta D'Aloi, who has collaborated with Julia, especially on her work with translation, and who is a laureate in languages at the University of Florence. Julia and Assunta invite us to sit at a simple wooden table. Julia tells us that we will be eating bread and soup—"Hermit's fare," she explains. My daughter and I will later hear from Julia about her affiliation with an Anglican order, Hermits of the Holy Family, an affiliation that enables her to watch after the cemetery while pursuing her scholarship and that explains her simple habit (a scarf and a long, loose-fitting dress). Much of her time and energy has been filled of late by an international collaboration on Dame Julian of Norwich, but she has found time to prepare a supper and to talk with my daughter and me about Latini.

The "bread" turns out to be a Tuscan specialty, "crostini," spread with a liver pate. Julia then ladles out large bowls of leek soup to supplement the bread, our simple but delicious dinner illuminated by candle light. The conversation immediately turns to Latini, and I am frustrated that I do not have my tape recorder turned on, so rich is what Julia has to say. The purpose of the evening is an "interview" that I proposed some time ago in an email message, but already, as we eat, I feel that I am in the presence not of a "subject," but of a gifted teacher, whose dinner-table conversation is filled with stories, learning, and laughter. The formality of an interview suddenly seems absurd to me, and I endeavor to listen as carefully as possible and to learn as much as I can. (A more formal interview, along with a viewing of Julia's collection of copies of Latini manuscripts, will occur later in Julia's study and library, but it is at dinner that I learn the most.)

Julia asks questions of both Amy and me, as does Assunta, who is seated with us. Julia tells us of her current work and suggests that we might collaborate with her. I tell her that I am not a medievalist, that my own work will involve introducing her work, and the work upon which it is "palimpsested," to use Julia's own scholarly vocabulary, to my home community of rhetoricians and teachers of writing. Julia seems somewhat embarrassed, and she is quick to credit others with what she knows. And yet, as the conversation continues, I begin to understand that these "others" are not only contemporary scholars, but also the textual voices of Dante, Latini, and Villani, voices who still speak not only in published Books, but also in archives. Julia has dwelled in archives for many years, and it quickly becomes clear that her understanding of Latini is built upwards. At the bottom are primary documents, letters, and illuminations; then there are the early Florentine histories; and finally there are the books and articles and translations done by other medievalists in a variety of disciplines. The collaboration in which Julia herself has participated seems daunting to me, one that is anything but second-hand.

As I eat a second bowl of leek soup—so soothing on a cold night—I watch myself listening. It is as though I am looking down from a distance, from the high ceiling of the Gatehouse kitchen. How will I remember all of this—all of the understanding of Latini that Julia so generously shares? I decide, in a kind of "meta" way, that I will endeavor to envision *alberi,* that I will use a strategy for remembering and sorting out information that Latini himself used and theorized. And so, even before the formal interview begins, I imagine categories. These categories do not correspond, exactly, to the questions I had jotted down in advance, hoping that they might guide the conversation. Indeed, they seem to grow from the conversation, more of a living tree than an outline. Although Julia Holloway is reluctant to emphasize her own story, her own career, I envision a bit of her story as an important category.

What are these categories, these emphases? I imagine them as I listen, and I know that they will serve as a map during my "interview" with Julia Holloway:

- Julia's story
- Latini's obscurity and the revival of interest in him
- Latini and orality
- Latini and literacy
- Latini as rhetorician
- Latini and the canon of arrangement
- Latini and a curriculum for ethical and mediatory applications of rhetoric

Michael Kleine

Although I earlier treated these topics rather indirectly in the literature review I wrote before coming to Florence, I now endeavor to foreground them since they grow from the words, which are present and living, of a remarkable scholar and human being.

Julia's Story

In the course of the meal, my daughter and I learn that Julia Holloway made some difficult career choices. Disturbed by departmental politics and the corporatizing devaluation of scholarship in American universities, she struck out on her own, pursuing a variety of scholarly and spiritual interests, often with very little institutional support. Her prolific scholarship led, at last, to her present appointment as Curator of the English Cemetery. After our evening with Julia, my daughter and I discussed the great impulse toward sharing and collaboration that is at the heart of all that Julia does. When she discovered that my daughter worked for Syracuse University in Florence, Julia expressed the hope that Syracuse students would avail themselves of her magnificent library, which includes copies of manuscripts in Latini's own hand.

Following dinner, Julia invites my daughter and me to visit her library, where she has set out copies of Latini's manuscripts in advance of our coming.

After showing us these copies, and their wonderful illuminations, Julia comments on why she became interested in Latini:

> *I began by writing a dissertation on Dante, Langland, and Chaucer. And in the process of that I discovered Brunetto Latini's poem,* Il Tesoretto. *Some years later I decided to edit* Il Tesoretto *as a published book. And it was an enchanting poem, filled with laughter.*

Illumination 14: Julia Holloway with a copy of Latini's Book.

> *The manuscript I chose to edit is a very beautiful, illuminated one, in which one can hear the people talking to each other, as if they are present—flesh and blood among the laughter. Then, later, I continued to come to Florence from America, where I was teaching, to work on the manuscripts. Almost every document that Brunetto writes—it was as if I were finding my way back into the text of*

> *Dante. Then I gave up on Brunetto. Now all of a sudden, everyone is becoming interested in him.*

LATINI'S OBSCURITY AND THE REVIVAL OF INTEREST IN HIM

Julia laments Brunetto's obscurity among American rhetoricians. (She calls him by his first name: it is as though she has something of a personal friendship with the long-dead Florentine notary and rhetorician.) She explains Brunetto's obscurity in this way:

> *Brunetto was, of course, tarred by Dante. And I now believe that there is some basis for the kind of tarring he received. In the past, the perception was that if you studied Latini, you were probably gay. And what in the world was a woman doing studying him? However, his manuscripts have been preserved by major European libraries, and he was enormously influential in his day. He is so modern. He deserves to be studied.*

Julia is reluctant to dwell on the possibility that Latini was gay, believing that his sexual orientation is beside the point. Instead, she focuses on his great contributions to Florence, the Renaissance, and rhetorical history in general.

She credits the revival of interest in Latini to his enormous impact on learning and writing during his day, and to the dramatic results of his teaching:

> *It was Brunetto who helped Dante understand how to create a Book. There are many different facets to Brunetto: he was, after all, the creator of not only the allegorical poem*

that influenced Dante, but also the creator of an encyclopedia and a rhetoric.

Especially, Julia emphasizes the importance of interdisciplinary collaboration to the revival of Latini studies, and to the accessibility and understanding of his manuscripts:

> *There has been much interdisciplinary collaboration. Art historians, for instance, have helped us understand manuscript illumination.*

It is telling that Julia does not credit herself for the revival of interest in Latini. One senses in her conversation, as in her writing, a very real humility. However, it is Julia's work with translation and explication that has enabled scholars and students to gain access, in English, to not only *Il Tesoretto*, but also Latini's notarial documents and letters. She models the kind of intellectual humility that both Latini and Dante valued, but sometimes failed to enact.

Latini and Orality

It does not come as a surprise to me when Julia says that she had found the writing of Father Walter Ong, especially *Orality and Literacy*, to be most helpful in her work. My own researching and teaching of writing has been influenced by Ong, and Julia's frequent use of the words "orality" and "presence" in her scholarly writing suggests Ong's influence. She expresses her sadness over Ong's recent death, and she then explains that his perspective on orality applies powerfully to medieval texts, including the texts written by Latini. For both Latini and Dante, the text was still close to the speaking voice, and reading the text aloud was part of the full hermeneutical process. Even Biblical texts were "heard" as living human voices. For Latini, then, Books were alive, and the written word was "present" in a context that was both immediate and rhetorical:

> *Medieval readers read aloud. Brunetto read aloud to his students, and the reading was present for his students, including Dante. The characters in the Books—Ovid, for instance, in* Il Tesoretto—*are very real, not only for Latini, but also for his students. And the Book is very real. When Dante meets Beatrice in the* Purgatorio, *she is surrounded by the Books of the Bible, who are all people. For them, the book was a human voice. The red rubrication was the red of blood—not at all an abstract color.*

As a teacher, Brunetto would have linked both the hearing and reading of the Book with the speaking and the writing of the Book. Thus,

> *Brunetto's students were encouraged not only to read, but to write, to play off the texts they were hearing and reading.*

Julia helps me see, in Brunetto Latini, an early practitioner of what we might call, today, a "whole-language" approach to teaching—speaking and hearing, writing and reading coming together in a classroom in which the Book, not the teacher, is centered.

Latini and Literacy

But Brunetto was also a great proponent of alphabetic, vernacular literacy. Indeed, Julia emphasizes his advocacy of an accessible and empowering literacy. In her discussion of the great contributions Brunetto made to Florentine democracy and cultural progress, she speaks with passion about

Latini's nearly liberatory emphasis on making both sacred and secular texts available to ordinary people:

> *Without the alphabet and without the Bible (neither of which is European), Europe would have had no lasting culture.*

Indeed, Julia's own work comprehends agendas that are decidedly liberatory and feminist:

> *In my own library here we have had a gypsy mother who has been copying out things, but she is still having difficulty learning to write and read. Her people, who are illiterate, had been slaves for many centuries in Romania. Illiteracy is a form of slavery. With literacy, "voices" are available that might provide empowerment. During the middle ages, many women, especially those in the convents, were literate, thanks to their self-teaching. And it was literacy that ultimately empowered women.*

As we listen to Julia, my daughter and I hear the words of a scholar who is committed, absolutely, not only to knowledge, but also to praxis that might reach out to those who are at the margins of literacy and power.

Latini as Rhetorician

Throughout our conversation, Julia stresses that Latini's work as a rhetorician cannot be separated from his democratic ideology and his sense of rhetoric's connection with judicial and political praxis. Latini was, like his own textual mentor, Cicero, a brilliant public speaker, one with a great sense of humor, and his public oratory effectively advanced in Florence and elsewhere the democratic values that he held:

> *Cicero, of course, was an advocate of government by the people. Latini, too, was interested in a government in which the people might participate. Brunetto was an effective orator: when he would speak, everyone would listen. Brunetto was clearly adapting Cicero to his own moment in time, incarnating and reincarnating Cicero in Florence. Brunetto was a humanist rhetorician during the middle ages, long before the Renaissance.*

Laughing, Julia tells us that Brunetto's brother was as ineffective as Brunetto was effective, bumbling through public addresses with little sense of focus and organization.

LATINI AND THE CANON OF ARRANGEMENT

Before my daughter and I dined with Julia, I had thought that it was Cicero's six-part approach to arrangement, advanced in *De Inventione,* that had best served Latini's public speaking, his letter writing, and even his literary efforts. Julia, however, passes quickly over the six-part structure and focuses on Latini's use of *alberi,* of hierarchical trees, in both the invention and disposition of his extended discourse, especially *Li Livres dou Tresor.* Indeed, she comments that Latini used a kind of "hyper-textual" approach to remembering, knowing, and writing:

> *I was fascinated when I was working with Brunetto's manuscripts, because in them he has these bubbles and lines. He carefully strategizes, visually, spatially, the arguments. These trees, these alberi—it's an organic form that he uses. It's not a pyramid;*

Julia Bolton Holloway

> *it's more the natural structure of a tree. It follows the structure of the mind, of memory. It is not an artificial structure. The way he structures a book, with the chapter headings at the beginning—everything follows through. In* Li Livres dou Tresor, *he begins with an encyclopedia and then moves toward a rhetoric, all intended to provide instruction for the podesta.*

Once again, Julia emphasizes Brunetto's constant focus on instruction—on the arrangement and presentation of knowledge deeply connected to his view of good governance and civic responsibility.

Latini and a Curriculum for Ethical and Mediatory Applications of Rhetoric

I have been endeavoring to provide short quotes of what Julia said to my daughter and me in relationship to the key topics that emerged during our conversation. Below, however, I will present the full interchange regarding Latini's impulse toward a curriculum for teaching rhetoric, a curriculum that seems decidedly modern in its emphasis on mediation and negotiation. I do this because I believe the conversational interchange below suggests the relational and new-rhetorical style of Julia herself.

Michael: As I read *Li Livres dou Tresor,* I had the sense that it was, almost, a curricular arrangement, beginning as it does with an encyclopedia, then providing an ethics, and finally concluding with advice concerning rhetoric and politics.
Julia: Yes. And it's wonderful teaching your ruler ethics before rhetoric.
Michael: We need that in America.

Michael Kleine

Julia: We need that all over the world.

Michael: Many American rhetoricians—I include myself—are interested in non-agonistic, cooperative rhetorics.

Julia: Excellent.

Michael: Such rhetorics are not so much concerned with "winning," but with constructing knowledge cooperatively.

Julia: Yes. Collaboration is one of the most important aspects of scholarship.

Michael: In reading Latini, I got the sense that he had a more or less mediatory impulse, especially in the construction of the treaties.

Julia: Florence and Siena, of course, had been great enemies. But Latini's work earned him the respect of the enemies of Florence. Secretly, Latini was interested in working with other cities, not against them. Brunetto was a brilliant negotiator.

In this transcription, one can almost hear Julia's marvelous teaching voice. It is a voice that does not dominate, does not lecture. Instead, it is a voice that supports and supplements what the student is trying to say, trying to clarify. It is a voice that shares in the construction of knowledge, never pontificating, always connected to the human subjectivity of both the teacher and the student. As I speak with Julia, I wonder if this is the way Latini and Dante interacted when, "from time to time," they spoke with one another.

The interview concludes when I ask Julia what she believes to be Latini's most significant contribution as a teacher of writing:

> *Latini encouraged the play of voices in writing. It is very important that we have a voice, and Latini helped his students understand how their own voices might be included in both letters and Books.*

I understand, of course, that Julia is talking about not only Latini, but also herself and me and my daughter. I have been her student for one evening, and I have been encouraged both to speak and, now, to write. In the presence of Julia's voice I find the Latini for whom I have been searching, and in her words I hear the words of Latini himself, words that might teach me how to write a Book of my own, close to the human lifeworld and close to the voices that are teaching me, a book filled with, if not illuminations, at least photographs.

Our visit with Julia Holloway does not end when I shut off my tape recorder. She wants to show Amy and me current work she is doing on the web. We move to a dim room next to Julia's library, in which her computer is centered.

Illumination 15: Julia Holloway, a medievalist for the twenty-first century.

Julia than proceeds to show us work in progress, a web page that, when she secures permissions, will include important Latini manuscripts that are for the time being hidden away in archives. On the computer screen, illuminated pages are magnified, every detail of the parchment clearly visible. Indeed, one will be able to see, even, the way text is sometimes palimpsested on text. Julia can hardly contain her excitement over the web project: she explains that her work, once completed, will enable scholars all over the world to observe and discuss electronically key Latini manuscripts. It seems so very fitting that Julia is positioning Latini's work, his great impulse to share knowledge and to include others, in such a way that others might see what she has seen in the archives of Florence and Rome. And it seems fitting that at the heart of contemporary access to Latini there will be links, nodes of *alberi,* hierarchically organized in relationship to other *alberi.* For what is the web if not a great, hypertextual tree, exactly the kind of tree, with open access to all, that Brunetto Latini imagined during the thirteenth century? Julia enacts and embodies the kind of literacy that Brunetto would have applauded.

Walking back to my daughter's apartment down a lantern-lit, winding street, narrow and paved with stones, I think that, yes, Latini himself might have wandered down this street, a street still available to Julia in her everyday life and a street available to me in my pilgrimage. I know that I have come home. I am a student again. And my teacher is a student. And her teacher was a student. And his. And his. And so on. All of the books that I have read before coming here now seem infolded in the spoken words of Julia Holloway, who had only recently been present in both being and language. All manner of thing seems well.

6 Homecoming and an Open Book

The rest of my trip to Florence is relatively uneventful. I chat with my daughter, and her friend, Roberto, about the great rivalry that still exists between Italian cities. Roberto seems disappointed when I tell him how much I enjoyed visiting Lucca, for he believes that it is his own city, Florence, and the hills surrounding it, that provided the language that is the basis for "the true Italian." As far as Roberto is concerned, other cities of Italy, and even of Tuscany, speak "dialects." Florentine Italian, after all, was the language of Dante—and of Dante's teacher, Latini, Roberto adds, knowing that I have been searching for Latini in particular. Roberto and Amy drive me to the airport, and in less than a full day I am back in the United States. I experience something like reverse culture shock upon arriving in Atlanta: the overall pace of experience seems accelerated; the physical space between people seems exaggerated and carefully maintained; the choice of airport eateries is overwhelming. I opt for fast-food Chinese and eat it near a television monitor showing the latest incidents in Iraq before finding my short flight home to Little Rock.

Back in Little Rock, I wonder how I will reach closure in terms of this Book. Cicero, I think, and also Latini, would recommend some sort of an action-oriented close, a more or less deliberative peroration—especially if I had in fact written, to this point, an argument, an academic treatise. But my search for Latini has been more a journey of discovery, something other than a strategically planned tour. My writing to this point, which has been a pilgrim's tale, now urges me to see it as an odyssey. Whereas Dante's dream journey ended at a point other than his point of departure, as did Latini's, I find myself back where I started. Dante's life ended in exile, but I am faced with the problem of homecoming, and of living and teaching on in a familiar country. Thus, I cannot look to Dante, or even to his teacher, Latini, for advice about how to end this particular Book. The only direction for me now seems to be a backward-looking one, a consideration of where I've already traveled and what I learned from my travel. From such reflective retrospection, perhaps, will come a conclusion, perhaps even a recommendation for future action.

Like my writing students at times, I am at a loss as to what I have said and what I mean, my "thesis" hidden, even from me, in my earlier wandering and drafting. I feel more like the Ancient Mariner than Latini, stopping my colleagues and even my students, trying, in an inarticulate way, to tell them where I have been, to tell them about searching for and, in a way I do not completely understand, finding Latini. Andrea Herrmann, my colleague and friend, stops me in the middle of a sentence: she tells me that I need a "writing conference," that I need to work out, now, just what I mean; who my audience is; what my purpose is. She is a good colleague, a good writing teacher, and she confronts me with hard questions rather than a glib assessment or insincere support of the journey and the Book about which I am babbling.

"Michael," she asks, "what is your point? What are you trying to say."

I like the way she says "say" rather than "write." "Yes, I respond, that's it—I am trying to say something about saying something."

She looks at me with sympathy, and she persists: "What in the world does *that* mean?"

"I mean," I say, " that I have something to say, but I am not sure what it is. I have written about my search for Latini, and I guess what I'm trying to say is this: we need to say more about him."

"Who is *we*?" she encourages.

"We is *us*. I mean, we who teach writing and we who care about—well, rhetoric. I mean to say, that is, we who are obscure, but who endeavor to provide for our students something other than obscurity."

She is silent, not knowing how to respond to what must seem like complete nonsense.

I take her silence as a question about Latini's significance. "After all," I blurt out, "he was the teacher of Dante! He was the first to translate Aristotle and Cicero into a vernacular language! He was damned by his teacher! And none of us, that is to say none of us who teach rhetoric in America, seem to know anything about him. He does not show up in our versions of rhetorical history. But others know much. Julia Holloway, for instance. She has much to say to us—and we need to listen."

"Why?" she asks. "Why should we care?"

"Because—well, because he has great rhetorical advice to offer about writing. Because he was an advocate of a decidedly liberatory pedagogy. Because he was a pioneer in writing to mediate and negotiate. Because he had a nearly hypertextual vision of knowledge. Because he probably influenced our Declaration of Independence and our Constitution. Most of all [. . .]"—I pause here, at a loss for the most important reason for caring—"because [. . .] he deconstructed master discourses and opened up the floor to voices that might have been silenced otherwise."

"So," Andrea probed, becoming suddenly Rogerian, "you're concerned about voices."

"Yes! Voices of resistance! Voices of the people."

"And you think," she continued, "that having a voice in writing might enable one to transcend—what?—what you call 'obscurity'?"

"Exactly. As Julia Holloway told me, it was literacy that gave women during the middle ages, especially those in the convents, a space in which to speak, to be heard."

"But I still don't see why we should know about Latini when, in fact, we already know about the importance of literacy in giving voice to those who are at the margins of power, who are even oppressed."

I was stumped. I had been trying to assert the potential importance of Latini to American rhetoricians and teachers of writing, but I had not yet gotten at his unique relevance to what we are trying to do in the here and now. Frustrated, I sputtered out, "It is the searching for Latini that matters! It is the searching for others who, like Latini, help us understand what we are trying to do when we teach writing."

"Are you saying that the point of all that you have done is personal, that it has restored your sense of the value of teaching writing and clarified your own sense of teacherly purpose?"

"Yes. That's it exactly."

"Now you're talking," Andrea said, and turned away toward the demands of her own scholarship and teaching.

༄

Thanks to my writing conference with my colleague, I understand better what it is that I have been trying to say. In the end, my point is a personal one, but one that might speak to all of us who endeavor to teach writing to others.

Homecoming and an Open Book

Searching for Latini, and *Searching for Latini,* has taught me to write my own Book. My end must be my beginning, my Apocalypse my Genesis. My earlier pages both lamented and valued the obscurity of Latini, the obscurity of the writing teacher. And yet, my lament has provided me with something to say, has enabled me, at least in a small way, to transcend my sense of personal obscurity. Indeed, Latini has restored to me a sense of voice and of knowing why it is that I teach writing, teaching that I have done in a rather automatic way for the past thirty years: I teach writing because I deeply believe that it enables democratic praxis, that it offers to those who might otherwise feel voiceless a sense of voice and presence in the face of discursive forces that work, powerfully, to silence little voices, small voices, the voices of the people. I am certain, as I move toward the final words of my own Book, that I will return to the teaching of writing with renewed energy and passion. I am certain that I will better understand, during the remaining days of my teaching, what it is I am trying to do and why I am trying to do it.

Along the steps of my pilgrimage, I have found important guides—Max, my own daughter, and Julia Bolton Holloway—and thanks to their guidance I have moved from the Inferno of obscurity and pointlessness to the Paradise of homecoming, of believing in the importance of my own praxis as both writer and teacher. For it is in traveling, in searching, that I have returned to a sense of belief and conviction. Another voice begins to speak to me, the voice of a former student, Matthew Abraham, who completed his doctorate in rhetoric and writing at Purdue University and now teaches at DePaul. Matthew's dissertation and now the articles he is publishing urge the importance of seeing and practicing writing as a form of resistance. Over the past few years, I have followed Matthew's principled and passionate efforts to remind other writing teachers of the primacy of such a purpose, and I have admired his courage in confronting corporatizing impulses within American universities. He has personally resisted temptations to promote writing as a way of conducting business as usual. Now, after searching for Latini, I understand that Matthew has been speaking to (and about) my own lethargy, my own uncritical acceptance of writing's dark side, its potential to promote the interests and agendas of the powerful, the wealthy, and most of all the smug. In fact, I know that now I must listen more carefully to Matthew and others like him, that I must join with those who, often at risk of their own careers, work to promote a literacy that is decidedly critical, one that relentlessly interrogates its own motives and that endeavors to remain open to marginalized voices.

In order to teach writing, I must become a student again. And I must palimpsest my own teaching on the texts, the voices, of others who have been forces of resistance and of open discourse. My search for Latini has provided me with both energy and reassurance: there have been other teachers who have endeavored to write Books that do not close down discourse, but that open it up. Latini wrote such Books; Julia Bolton Holloway has written such Books; Matthew is now writing such Books. For myself, and perhaps for all of us who teach writing, the implication seems strong: the writing teacher might be a force of what I want to call, at last, "The Open Book." For it is the Open Book—the Book in which the voices of the people speak, in which the end is in fact the beginning—that advances a human and living discourse of resistance, inclusion, presence, and authenticity. Julia Holloway had reminded me that the best kind of scholarship endeavors to share knowledge, to open up the construction of knowledge to collaboration and inclusive discussion. And so I come to understand that it is not the search for Latini, or whatever it is that he might represent, that matters greatly to me as a writer and as a teacher; it is, instead, the way in which we search for Latini, the spirit of our search, that most matters. I want to believe that Latini himself understood what I am groping to say here, that he would have celebrated with me not those manuscripts written in Latin and hidden away in archives, but the living, speaking texts that advance, in the vernacular, words that are palimpsested on the words of others, words that are available to all.

A recommendation? An action-oriented close? I do not have one to give, now. My final speech act must be more of an invitation than a directive, more of an opening than a closing. I invite others to join Julia Bolton Holloway, my mentor, and others in the search for Latini. And now it is time to be silent, in hope that other voices might enter and transform what I have been calling my " Book," which I see at last as less of a Book than a turn in a conversation that is as old as rhetoric itself. And it is time, now, to turn back to my own teaching with the sense that Latini is ghosted beside me, as he is ghosted beside Dante in Giotto's fresco, and that I am part of a great, liberatory tradition, a tradition that defies tradition, and part of a historically constituted community that is, in its sharing and collective speaking, anything but obscure.

Works Cited

Primary Sources

Alighieri, Dante. *The Divine Comedy*. Trans. by Allen Mandelbaum. New York: Everyman's Library, 1995.

Latini, Brunetto. *La rettorica*. Quaderno di Letteratura e d'Arte. n.s., 23. Ed. Francesco Maggini. Preface, Cesare Segre. Florence: Le Monnier, 1968.

—. *Il tesoretto*. Garland Library of Medieval Literature, 2. Ed. and trans. Julia Bolton Holloway. New York: Garland, 1981.

—. *The Book of the Treasure (Li Livres dou Tresor)*. Ed. and translated by Paul Barrette and Spurgeon Baldwin. New York: Garland Publishing, 1993.

—. *Li livres dou Tresor de BL*. Ed. Francis J. Carmody. Berkeley: U of California P, 1947. Rpt Geneva: Slatkine, 1975.

Villani, Filippo. *Liber de civitatis Florentiae famosis civibus*. Ed. G. C. Galetti. Florence, 1847.

Villani, Giovanni. *Cronica di Giovanni Vallani*. Ed. F. Gherardi Dragomanni. *Collezione di storici e cronisti italani editi ed inedti*, vol. 1–4. Florence, 1844–45.

Secondary Sources

Burke, Kenneth. *A Rhetoric of Motives*. 1950. Berkeley: U of California P, 1969.

Camille, Michael. "The Pose of the Queer: Dante's Gaze, Brunetto Latini's Body." *Queering the Middle Ages*. Ed. Glen Burger and Seven F. Kruger. Minneapolis: U of Minnesota P, 2001, 57–86.

Dole, Nathan Haskan. *A Teacher of Dante and Other Studies in Italian Literature*. New York: Moffatt, Yard, 1908.

Works Cited

Colish, Marcia L. *The Mirror of Language: A Study in the Medieval Theory of Knowledge*. New Haven: Yale UP, 1968.

East, James Robert. "Brunetto Latini's Rhetoric of Letter Writing." *Quarterly Journal of Speech* 54 (1968): 241–46.

Freire, Paulo. *Pedagogy of the Oppressed*. Trans. Myra Bergman Ramos. New York: Continuum, 1982.

Flower, Linda. *Problem-Solving Strategies for Writing*. New York: Harcourt, Brace Jovanovich, Inc., 1981.

Holloway, Julia Bolton. *Brunetto Latini: An Analytic Bibliography*. London: Grant and Cutler, Ltd., 1986.

—. "Chancery and Commedy: Brunetto Latini and Dante." *Lectura Dantis* 3 (Fall 1988) 7 Sep. 2003 <http://www.brown.edu/Departments/Italian_Studies/LD/numbers/03.html>.

—. Introduction. *Il Tesoretto*. Garland Library of Medieval Literature, 2. Ed. and trans. Julia Bolton Holloway. New York: Garland, 1981.

—. *The Pilgrim and the Book*. New York: Peter Lang, 1987.

—. *Twice-Told Tales*. New York: Peter Lang, 1993.

Jauss, Hans Robert. "The Alterity and Modernity of Medieval Literature." *New Literary History* 10 (1979): 173–92.

Kay, Richard. *Dante's Swift and Strong: Essays on* Inferno *XV*. Lawrence: Regents Press of Kansas, 1978.

Kermode, Frank. *The Sense of an Ending*. New York: Oxford UP, 1967.

Ong, Walter. *Orality and Literacy: The Technologizing of the Word*. New York: Routledge, 1988.

Index

Abbot Tesauro, 25, 26, 99
Abraham, Matthew, 127, 128
ad hominem 79
Adam, 49
alberi (see also trees), 50, 55, 68, 77, 88, 111, 118–119, 122
Alexander the Great, 35
American rhetorical canon, 9, 11; as living baseball game, 11
American rhetoricians, 5, 11, 13, 19, 29, 32, 60, 65, 66, 73, 77, 88–89, 95, 114, 120, 126
Ancient Mariner, 87, 124
Aristotle, 5, 21, 24, 27, 28, 44, 47, 52, 59, 71, 72, 74, 75, 87, 88, 125; Aristotelian virutes, 34, 77
arrangement (see also rhetoric: canons of), 68, 77, 81–82, 88, 111, 118–119
ars dictaminis, 48, 80–82, 88
Athens, 23, 30
Atlanta, 123
audience, 32; and Cicero, 35, 68, 81–82; and Latini, 34, 35, 37, 68, 69, 71, 77, 81–82; of Kleine, 124

Baldwin, Spurgeon, 66–70
Battle of Montaperti, 21, 25–27, 33
Beatrice, 6, 49, 116
Bible, the, 7, 26, 30, 50, 73, 115, 116, 117
Boethius, 37, 49
Book: of Dante, 9, 42, 110, 114; of Holloway, 7, 8, 9, 38, 109, 128; of Kleine, 9, 12–13, 37, 43, 60, 62–63, 66, 87, 93, 95, 121, 123–124, 127, 129; of Latini, 8, 9, 12, 26–30, 33, 36, 38, 42, 46, 50, 59, 60, 110, 114–116, 120, 128; of Matthew, 26, 30, 60
Botticelli, 17
Browning, Elizabeth Barrett, 109
Burke, Kenneth, 9

Camille, Michael, 52
Carmody, 66
Catalina, 22, 30
Cato, 30, 74
Chaucer, 7, 112
Chiamenti, Massimiliano, 3, 4, 5, 88, 127

Index

Cicero: and audience, 35, 68, 81–82; and Latini, 4, 5, 21, 22, 24, 25, 26, 27, 28, 30, 32, 35, 37, 38, 46, 51, 59, 60, 63, 66–67, 70–74, 77–82, 86, 87, 88, 100–101, 117, 118, 125; and Dante, 49, 52, 57, 59–60; as rhetor, 3, 4, 10, 22, 26, 29, 38, 51, 52, 62, 70, 72, 74, 75, 77–82, 107, 117, 123; Ciceronian friend, 35; politics of, 18–19, 28, 51, 52, 57, 59, 70, 74, 77, 81, 100, 118
Colish, Marcia, 47, 51
Columbus, 6
collaboration, 11, 19, 109, 110–112, 115, 120, 128
composition, 22, 29, 32, 50, 73, 80, 82
consubstantiality, 9
Corax, 27, 77

D'Aloi, Assunta, 109, 110
Dante, 3, 4, 7, 9, 11, 12, 13, 20, 24, 26, 32, 33, 67, 110, 112, 114, 115, 124; ambivalence toward Latini, 42–44; and politics, 10, 43–44, 46, 48, 52–55, 56–57, 59–60, 63; and Virgil, 52, 59; as copyist, 42–43; as student of Latini, 3, 4, 5, 11, 12, 19, 20, 23, 27, 33, 37, 38, 39, 42, 42–63, 66, 80, 86–88, 93, 101, 102, 114–116, 120, 123; conception of human nature, 56–57; damnation of Latini, 4, 6, 11, 12, 26, 39–47, 49, 52–55, 60, 80, 105, 114, 125; dream vision of, 33, 48, 50, 51, 124; gratitude to Latini, 41, 44, 45; in Inferno, 3, 39–44, 52, 54–56, 57, 59, 63, 105; memorials of, 4, 101–103, 129
Davidsohn, Lascito, 89
De Inventione, 19, 28, 62, 66, 67, 81, 82, 118
Declaration of Independence, 89, 125
deconstruction, 29, 32, 35, 36
Democracy, 17, 21, 23, 29, 35, 61, 68, 69, 79, 100, 116
discourse, and democracy, 10, 66, 71, 73, 79, 85, 89; and power, 23, 27, 71, 97, 126, 128; chancery, 22, 25–27; graffiti as, 96–99; political, 30, 87, 96; public, 61, 73, 81, 97, 99;
Divine Comedy, The, 4, 6, 7, 12, 26, 47, 48, 50, 65, 97; the Inferno (see also Inferno, the), 3, 6, 12, 20, 39–42, 44, 46, 51, 55, 59, 63, 105, 127; Paradise, 6, 12, 33, 55, 59, 61, 63, 87, 93, 127; Purgatory, 12, 52, 93, 116
Dole, Nathan Haskin, 27, 37, 38, 50
dream vision: of Cicero, 32; of Dante, 33, 48, 50, 51, 124; of Kleine, 93, 124; of Latini, 31–37, 51, 124
Dream of Scipio, 32

134

Index

East, James, 66, 80
encyclopedia, 9, 26, 27, 30, 31, 32, 33, 37, 49, 50, 67, 69, 79, 115, 119
England, 11, 19
English Cemetery, 7, 104, 108–112
Epistolorium, the, 22, 24, 28, 42, 88
ethos, 10, 31, 72
Etruscans, 43, 95
exile: of Dante, 49, 87, 124; of Kleine, 6–10, 18, 87, 88, 95, 124; of Latini, 6–10, 18, 21, 22, 24–28, 33, 37, 52, 65, 87

fame, 31, 35, 37, 41, 48–49, 53, 55, 57–58
Farinata, 30
feminism, 117
Field of Dreams, 11
Florence, 3–8, 10, 11, 13, 17, 18, 19, 21, 25, 27, 29, 30, 38, 40, 43, 47, 53, 66, 86, 89, 93, 94, 95, 97, 98, 100, 104, 105, 109, 112, 113, 114, 118, 120, 122, 123; Piazza Della Signoria, 99; Santa Croce, 4, 95, 97, 101, 103; the Duomo, 17, 95–97, 103; Uffizi, the, 95, 100; University of, 13, 109
Flower, Linda, 50
Fortune, 41, 49
France, 9, 27, 31, 41, 67
Francessco d'Accorso, 41, 55
Freire, Paulo, 22, 61–62, 107

French, 4, 9, 19, 26, 27, 30, 37, 47, 48, 51, 53, 65, 67, 77

Galileo, 17, 97
Ghibellines, 18, 21–23, 25–27, 33, 47, 53, 99
Giamboni, Bono, 47
God, 33, 35, 36, 54–57, 59–60
Gorgias, 75
graffiti, 96–99, 107
Gran Tesoro, 24, 37–38, 42, 45, 47, 53, 58–59
Guelfs, 10, 18, 21, 22, 23, 25–28, 30, 33, 36, 37, 43, 55, 56, 60

Hermagoras, 76, 78, 79
Herrmann, Andrea, 124, 126
hierarchy, 12, 18, 28, 50, 55–57, 67, 69–71, 79, 88, 89, 93, 118, 122
Holloway, Julia Bolton, 7–13, 18–21, 23–30, 32, 34–36, 38, 43, 46–49, 51, 53, 61, 62, 65, 80, 86, 89, 104, 108–112, 114–122, 125–129
homecoming, 124, 127
humility, 33, 62–63, 115
hypertext, 50, 118, 122, 125

ideology, 18, 23, 30, 33, 52, 54, 60, 63, 68, 70, 71, 73, 74, 96, 117; and teaching writing, 46, 61
Il Tesoretto, 19, 26, 27, 29, 30–34, 36–38, 42, 46–51,

Index

53, 58, 112, 115–116
Inferno, the, 3, 6, 12, 20, 39–42, 44, 46, 51, 55, 59, 63, 105, 127
ink: brown, 20, 21, 27, 38, 44; purple, 20, 27, 38
intertextuality, 5, 10, 20, 25, 29, 30, 31, 36–37, 43, 47, 49, 50, 61, 73, 89, 96, 98
invention, 32, 68, 77, 118
Iraq, 96, 123
irony, 10, 27, 31–35, 45, 48, 99, 105

Jauss, Hans Robert, 31
Jerusalem, 23
Jesus Christ, 26, 32, 56
Julius Caesar, 35

kairos, 63, 72, 97
Kay, Richard, 53–61
Kermode, Frank, 7, 36
King Manfred, 21, 25, 27
Kleine, Amy, 3, 13, 19, 93, 95, 98, 104, 106, 108–110, 112, 117–123, 127
Kleine, Michael: Apocalypse of, 13, 127; as copyist, 43–45, 97; as student, 42, 43, 63, 79, 86, 121–122, 128; as teacher, 4, 5, 6, 9, 11, 12, 20, 45, 46, 52, 60–62, 86, 87, 95, 102, 103, 126, 127; exile of, 6, 7, 8, 9, 10, 18, 87, 88, 95, 124; genesis of 3, 9, 13, 127; pilgrimage of, 5, 6, 8, 9, 38, 46, 62, 86–88, 93, 95, 122–127;

La Penetenza, 35
La Rettorica, 19, 28–30, 50, 67
Latin, 3, 18, 22, 24, 25, 27, 29, 30, 50, 51, 55, 66, 67, 77, 129
Latini, Bianca, 19–21
Latini, Brunetto: and audience, 34, 35, 37, 68, 69, 72, 77, 81–82; and eloquence, 51, 68, 74; and orality 31–32, 47, 73, 80–81, 83, 111, 115–116; as ambassador, 18, 21, 25; as citizen of Florence, 18, 21, 93–94; as father, 19–21; as notary, 12, 18, 20, 21, 23, 25–29, 38, 114, 115; as rhetorician, 18, 20, 21, 24–27, 29–30, 32, 38, 45, 48, 49, 60, 62, 69–76, 88, 111, 114, 117–118, 125; as teacher, 3, 4, 5, 6, 7, 11, 12, 18, 19, 20, 27, 30, 33, 38, 42–49, 50, 52, 58, 59, 60, 62, 65, 66, 73, 74, 80, 86–89, 93, 95, 98, 100, 102, 105, 114, 116, 120, 125, 128; as translator, 22, 23, 28–29, 30, 71, 74, 81; as unstagnant fountain, 4, 60, 101; as writer, 20, 21, 24, 27, 38, 47, 57, 80–86, 93, 113, 128; banishment to hell, 4, 6, 11, 12, 26, 39–47, 49, 52–55, 60, 80, 105, 125; blasphemy of, 53–56; documents of, 24–38, 104, 112–115,

118, 121–122; dream vision of, 31–37, 51; exile of, 6, 7, 8, 9, 10, 18, 21, 22, 24–28, 33, 37, 52, 65, 87; in *Inferno*, 20, 37, 40–42; memorials of, 4, 11, 25, 38, 60, 100–104, 129; obscurity of, 5, 6, 8, 11, 12, 60, 65, 87–88, 101, 106, 111, 114, 127, 129; popularity of, 66–67; resistance of, 26, 34–35, 99; sins of, 36, 41, 42, 46, 48, 52–60; three-part plan of, 68–71; use of vernacular, 4, 18, 21–23, 27–30, 37, 47, 51, 53, 62, 65, 67, 71, 79, 87–89, 116; Via Latini, 105–107
Latini, Perseo, 20–21
Li Livres dou Tresor, 9, 19, 26–30, 33, 37, 38, 47–50, 54, 58–60, 62, 63, 65–74, 77, 79, 80, 83, 85, 88, 118, 119
literacy, 22–24, 62, 66, 73, 89, 111, 116, 117, 122, 126, 128
Logic, 69–70

Machiavelli, 17, 28, 97
map, 3, 105, 106; of *Inferno*, 12, 54; of Kleine's work, 8, 12, 111
Medici family, 17
memory, 32, 41, 44, 49–50, 119
mentor, 4, 6, 39, 42, 43, 44, 50–53, 58–60, 62, 68, 71, 72, 74, 86–88, 117, 129
Michelangelo, 17, 97, 99

naming, 19–20, 29, 55
Natura, 33, 34
Nicomachean Ethics, 28, 71, 72

obscurity: of Latini, 5, 6, 8, 11, 12, 60, 65, 87–88, 101, 106, 111, 114, 127, 129; of writing teacher, 5, 8, 11, 61, 103, 126–127
Odyssey, the, 7
Ong, Walter, 32, 115
Ovid, 37, 116

palimpsest, 19, 28–30, 43, 50, 60, 62, 63, 66, 71, 74, 77, 82, 86, 97, 107, 110, 122, 128
palinode, 35–36
Pass of Roncevalles, 21, 33, 53
pedagogy, 9, 46, 50, 58; banking, 62; liberatory, 22, 24, 62, 66, 73, 87, 89, 117, 125, 129; of imitation, 42; whole-language, 116
Petrarch, 3, 17
Pier delle Vigne, 22, 26
pilgrim: as creator within creation, 8, 114; Dante as, 8, 12, 46, 49, 51, 86; Kleine as, 5–12, 43, 46, 49, 51, 60, 63, 95, 124; Latini as, 46
pilgrimage, 36, 43, 50, 51, 54, 65; of Dante, 5, 6, 50, 86; of Kleine, 5, 6, 8, 9, 38, 46, 62, 86–88, 93, 95, 122–127; allegorical, 5, 19;

Index

guide through, 5, 6, 8, 12, 39, 40, 52, 54, 58, 62, 65, 79, 95, 108, 111, 127
Plato, 46, 60
poetry, 5, 43, 48, 50, 52, 97
politics: and Cicero, 18–19, 28, 51, 52, 57, 59, 70, 74, 77, 81, 100, 118; Italian, 17, 18, 23–24, 38, 29, 30, 32, 33, 48, 55, 57, 94, 95, 96, 98, 100; of Dante, 10, 43–44, 46, 48, 52–55, 56–57, 59–60, 63; of Latini, 5, 12, 18, 20, 21, 23, 24, 28–30, 32, 33, 44, 46, 48, 49, 51, 52, 57, 59, 61–62, 69–73, 77, 79–81, 83, 86–87, 117, 119; of teaching writing, 61–62
postmodernism, 29, 86, 89
practice, 69–70; political, 10, 17, 23, 30, 33, 70, 71, 79, 80, 83, 84; rhetorical, 13, 30, 31, 38, 52, 61, 71, 72, 75, 79, 80
praxis, 10, 18, 20, 21, 22, 24, 30, 57, 62, 77, 79, 88, 89, 117, 127
pride, 18, 22, 36, 46, 48, 49, 57–62
Primo Popolo, 21
Princeton University, 11
Ptolemy, 36–37
pun, 20, 25, 26, 30, 44

republican, 21, 28, 35, 44, 100; Cicero as, 10, 28, 29, 52; Latini as, 30, 33, 53, 59, 68, 74; republican values, 18, 37, 57, 62, 70–72; Roman Republic, 18, 21, 22, 43
rhetoric, 5, 129; and governance, 27, 59, 66, 74–79, 83, 88, 119; and Latini, 4, 5, 9, 24–32, 37–38, 44–49, 69–80, 100, 111, 114–117, and virtue, 72, 119; and writing, 5, 6, 9, 10, 12, 13, 19, 52, 60, 64, 65, 80, 86, 87, 127; bad use of, 59; canons of, 9, 11, 31, 65, 68, 73, 77, 81–82, 87, 88, 111, 118–119; ceremonial, 48, 77; classical, 5, 19, 26, 28, 67, 68, 70, 72, 73, 77, 82; controversy in, 81; deliberative, 10, 60, 62, 66, 77, 88, 96–97, 123; empowerment through, 27, 62, 66, 74, 117, 125; forensic, 10, 77, 88; oral, 23, 30, 31, 47, 71–75, 78, 80, 81, 83, 85, 115–116, 118, 128, 129; teacher of, 4, 6, 29, 38, 52, 86; written 80–86
Rogers, Carl, 126
Romans, 18, 19, 22, 29, 43, 55
Rome, 17, 21, 23, 30, 43, 122

Sallust, 30
Santa Maria Maggiore, 4, 11, 13, 25, 38, 100
Searching for Latini, 62, 127
Seventh Circle of Hell, the, 6, 39, 43, 54, 60, 86
Shakespeare, 5
Sicily, 25, 27

Siena, 17, 18, 25, 95, 120
social construction, 73, 120, 128
Socrates, 46
sodomy, 6, 39, 43, 45, 46, 52–54
sophists, 70, 74, 77
Spain, 21
stasis theory, 77
structuralism, 82
student, 42, 53, 112, 115, 120, 127; as copyist, 43, 45, 97; Dante as, 12, 23, 39, 43–48, 51–52, 58, 80, 86, 101, 102, 116; Kleine as, 42, 43, 63, 79, 86, 121–122, 128; Latini as, 51; of Latini, 27, 30, 33, 42, 43, 45, 47, 60, 73, 116, 120; writing students, 5, 10, 11, 45–46, 50, 60–62, 71, 89, 107, 112, 115, 120, 122, 124, 127

teacher of writing, 5, 6, 11, 12, 13, 45, 61–62, 65, 66, 77, 86, 87, 88, 89, 95, 103, 110, 120, 124, 126, 127; and ideology, 46, 61–62; and the Open Book, 128; as midwife, 8; decentralization of, 42, 116; desires of, 45; Kleine as, 4, 5, 6, 9, 11, 12, 20, 45, 46, 52, 60–62, 86, 87, 95, 102, 103, 126, 127; Latini as, 3, 4, 5, 6, 7, 11, 12, 18, 19, 20, 27, 30, 33, 38, 42–49, 50, 52, 58, 59, 60, 62, 65, 66, 73, 74, 80, 86–89, 93, 95, 98, 100, 102, 105, 114, 116, 120, 125, 128; obscurity of, 5, 8, 11, 61, 103, 126–127
travel narrative, 13, 95
treasure: earthly, 35, 49, 53, 60, 63, 64; Latini's work as, 12, 13, 21, 26, 30, 33, 35, 36, 47, 51, 53, 60, 63–65, 71, 72, 80
trees (See also *alberi*), 50, 55, 68, 111, 118–119, 122
Tuscany, 3, 4, 95, 123
Twice Told Tales, 19, 20, 21, 24, 28, 47, 49, 52, 89

United States Constitution, 10, 89, 125
University of Arkansas at Little Rock, 9, 123

Vatican, 19
vernacular, 4, 19, 21, 22, 47, 65, 89, 96, 107, 116, 125, 129; Latini's use of, 4, 18, 21–23, 27–30, 37, 47, 51, 53, 62, 65, 67, 71, 79, 87–89, 116
Via Latini, 105–107
Villani, Giovanni, 19, 38, 110
Virgil, 6, 39, 44, 52, 54, 57–59
virtue, 46, 48, 56, 67, 69, 72
voice, 24, 63, 74, 79, 87, 93, 96–97, 107, 110, 115–117, 120–121, 126–129

Werge, Thomas, 53

About the Author

Michael Kleine is a professor in the Department of Rhetoric and Writing at the University of Arkansas at Little Rock, where he teaches courses in first-year writing, composition theory, rhetorical theory, language theory, and science writing. In the summer of 2004, he taught a special-topics course on Brunetto Latini. His published articles have appeared in *Rhetoric Society Quarterly, Technical Communication Quarterly, Communication and Religion, Journal of Business and Technical Communication, JAC: A Journal of Composition Theory, Journal of Medical Humanities, Journal of Teaching Writing, The Writing Instructor, ex tempore* (a music-theory journal), the *Journal of Psychological Type, Centrum,* and *Composition Forum.* He has published book chapters in *The Philosophy of Discourse* and *(Re)Visioning Composition Textbooks.* He has also published poetry on Italian art and literature in *Poem* and *The Formalist.*

www.ingramcontent.com/pod-product-compliance
Lightning Source LLC
Chambersburg PA
CBHW031631160426
43196CB00006B/375